HOW TO ACE THE BRAINTEASER INTERVIEW

JOHN KADOR

MCGRAW-HILL

NEW YORK   CHICAGO   SAN FRANCISCO   LISBON   LONDON
MADRID   MEXICO CITY   MILAN   NEW DELHI   SAN JUAN
SEOUL   SINGAPORE   SYDNEY   TORONTO

The **McGraw·Hill** Companies

8 9 0 DSH/DSH 0 1 0 9 8 7 6 5

ISBN 0-07-144001-1

McGraw-Hill books are available at special quantity discounts to use as premiums and sales promotions, or for use in corporate training programs. For more information, please write to the Director of Special Sales, McGraw-Hill, Two Penn Plaza, New York, NY 10121-2298. Or contact your local bookstore.

This book is printed on recycled, acid-free paper containing a minimum of 50% recycled, de-inked fiber

To Peter and Robert, my brothers

CONTENTS

CONTENTS

PREFACE

Here's a brainteaser for you.

Why do employers subject already nervous job candidates to brainteasers, puzzles, business cases, and other mind-benders? Do such puzzles really help employers build teams of highly logical, curious, successful, hard-working, motivated contributors who can be expected to hit the ground running?

Hardly anyone believes that. There are no studies that give scientific support to the notion that success at brainteasers and logic puzzles predicts success at the job. So if employers know that, why do interviewers persist in using valuable job interview time for this peculiar style of interviewing?

Interviewers look to brainteasers to do one thing: to start a safe conversation that reveals how smart candidates are. Intelligence is seen as a critical predictor of success on the job, and brainteasers allow interviewers to get a measure of a candidate's intelligence. "There is a strong correlation between basic intelligence and success in software engineering," says Ole Eichorn, chief technical officer (CTO) of Aperio Technologies in Vista, California. "Unfortunately the forces of political correctness have taken away a key tool—employers can't give intelligence tests to candidates. In the meantime, puzzles are a decent proxy. By giving candidates good puzzles you get a fair estimate of how smart they are, and the discussion gives you some interaction with the candidate, too."

With the downturn in the tech sectors, more and more people are chasing fewer jobs. Interviewers are often faced with hundreds of résumés for one position. When all these candidates seem exceptionally qualified for the job, how is the interviewer to select? Using brainteasers and puzzles makes sense at companies that focus recruitment efforts more on what candidates might do in the future than on what they have done in the past. These companies understand that in today's fast-paced global business world, specific skills are of limited use because technology changes so quickly. What is really needed, interviewers believe, are curious, observant, quick-witted candidates who welcome new challenges, demonstrate mental agility under stressful conditions, learn quickly, defend their thinking, and demonstrate enthusiasm for impossible tasks.

It also doesn't hurt that Microsoft, the most successful company of all time, is known to add brainteasers to the mix of interview questions it asks the thousands of super-bright candidates who come knocking at its gates. No human resources director has ever been fired for aligning his or her company's hiring practices with Microsoft's.

PUZZLES AND BRAINTEASERS IN ACTION

Joel Spolsky, president of New York–based Fog Creek Software, understands that brainteasers or other challenges are a critical part of the interview process because they help narrow the large number of "maybes" that crowd any job search. "There are three types of people in the software field," notes Spolsky, who got his first job at Microsoft. "At one end of the scale, there are the unwashed masses, lacking even the most basic skills for the job." They are easy to ferret out and eliminate, often just by reviewing a résumé and asking two or three quick questions. At the other extreme are the superstars who write compilers for fun. "And in the middle, you have a large number of 'maybes' who seem like they might just be able to contribute something," Spolsky adds.

At Fog Creek, brainteasers are used to identify candidates who not only are smart, but who get things done. "Our goal is to hire people with *aptitude*, not a particular skill set," Spolsky says. "*Smart* is important, but hard to define; *gets things done* is crucial. In order to be able to tell, you're going to have to ask the right questions."

The brainteaser challenge comes after Spolsky establishes rapport with the candidate, asks about skills and projects, and poses some behavioral questions ("Tell me about a time when you faced a deadline crunch . . ."). The first thing Spolksy looks for in a candidate is passion.

After that, he gives the candidate an impossible gross-order estimation question. "The idea is to ask a question that they have no possible way of answering, just to see how they handle it," he says. How many optometrists are there in Seattle? How many tons does the Washington Monument weigh? How many gas stations are in Los Angeles? More of these puzzles can be found in Chapter 9.

"What an applicant knows gets him or her through the first interview," says Ed Milano, vice president of Marketing and Program Development at Design Continuum, a product design consulting firm with offices in Boston, Milan, and Seoul. By the time the applicant gets to Milano, aptitude and experience are not in question. For Milano to make a job offer, he has to see how the applicant thinks under stressful conditions, the environment that often describes life at a consultancy that assists clients with make-or-break strategic design programs.

Ed Milano, like many recruiters, has often found that starting an interview with a brainteaser is effective. Logic puzzles have a long tradition in fast-moving high-tech companies where being quick on your feet is an asset. As the rest of the world has embraced the attributes of the fast-moving, ever-wired, start-up mentality of the high-tech computer company, many recruiters are adopting the in-your-face style of interviewing associated with technology-intensive start-ups. Some recruiters earnestly believe that brainteasers are valid tools to gauge the creativity, intelligence, passion, resourcefulness, etc., of candidates. Others are willing to accept that puzzles are little more than interview stunts that may or may not reveal aspects of the candidate's character and may actually alienate some candidates. In any case, brainteasers are here to stay.

A reasonable question readers often ask me is, "Given that this book has now published these brainteasers and their solutions, why would any interviewer ever use these brainteasers again?"

Let me give two answers. First, interviewers love candidates who have prepared for interviews. They want you to prepare. The fact is, there are literally hundreds of Web sites that discuss these puzzles, sometimes with solutions, sometimes not. Besides, many of these brainteasers don't have solutions. And of the puzzles that do, interviewers understand, as you should, that reading the solutions to these puzzles is no substitute for understanding them and being able to carry on an intelligent conversation. And intelligent conversation—what these brainteasers are designed to catalyze—can't be faked.

Second, there are dozens of interviewing books that prep candidates on such staples of the job interview as "Where do you want to be in five years?" and "What's your greatest weakness?" but interviewers still ask those questions. You can buy this book with confidence. The next job interview brainteaser you are asked is likely to be discussed within these pages.

Good luck on acing the brainteaser job interview.

JOHN KADOR
Geneva, Illinois

ACKNOWLEDGMENTS

My gratitude goes, first, to those who advised me not to write this book. Some very smart people argued that it is neither valid nor moral to make brainteasers a part of the job selection process, but in making their case they contributed some very juicy brainteasers that made their way into this book. Whether we like it or not, job interview brainteasers are out there and we should be prepared. As Trotsky said, "You don't have to believe in street cars to take them where you want to go."

Dozens of other veterans of the brainteaser wars, not all of whom want to be named here, helped me compile these puzzles and their solutions. The brainteasers themselves were offered with generosity. The preferred solutions were held in greater confidence, and I am most grateful to those who occasionally bent a company policy or two to share their insights with me. I also acknowledge the workers who recounted their often exasperating experiences with brainteasers in the context of tension-filled job interviews. Whether they operate on one side of the interviewing table or the other, I am grateful to the following individuals who permitted me to mention their names: Peter Alkemade, Adam Barr, Phil Brady, Dale Fedderson, Robert Gately, Tom Gentry, Vikas Hamine, Charles Handler, Pete Herzog, Ben Kovler, Carl Kutsmode, Marie Lerch, Steve Levy, Joe Mabel, Bill McCabe, Ed Milano, Scott Schoenick, Kevin Stone, Koen Van Tolhuyzen, Kevin Wheeler, Jeffrey Yamaguchi.

Scores of Web logs (blogs) focus on the job interview process at Microsoft and other high-tech companies. A number of bloggers helped me define this book and invited their readers to contribute puzzles and personal experiences. This book is richer for their efforts. I would especially like to acknowledge the following individuals: Vicki Brown, Ole Eichorn, Ron Jacobs, Johanna Rothman, Chris Sells, Joel Spolsky, and Jeffrey Yamaguchi. Links to their blogs may be found in Appendix E.

Mr. Micah Fogel, an instructor in the math department at Illinois Math and Science Academy in Aurora, Illinois, agreed to recruit a couple of his top math students to review the puzzles in this book. IMSA (www.imsa.edu) is an elite, residential high school that attracts academically gifted students from throughout Illinois. I am indebted to Micah and his excellent students, Letian Zhang and Xi Ye, for making several suggestions that spared this book of critical lapses in logic and rigor.

Finally, I am grateful to my friends and associates in Illinois who tolerated my insistent pestering on questions of wording and meaning. Roger Breisch, a good friend who once taught high-school mathematics, was generous in reviewing my equations and proofs; Roger invariably improved both. I am also grateful to Barry Glicklich, Katherine Lato, Dan Kador, Elizabeth Nelson, and David W. Jones for critical contributions to selected puzzles. Any errors, misstatements, or omissions in the presentation and unraveling of these puzzles, then, are entirely my own.

TO THE READER

If you are in the job market—particularly pursuing jobs in high tech, consulting, finance, insurance, and manufacturing—this book is for you. This book presents the largest collection of the actual puzzles, brainteasers, and mind-benders being used by interviewers and recruiters around the world. Many puzzles are printed here for the first time. With each puzzle is a discussion of not only the solution, but—more important—the quality of responses that interviewers find most compelling.

The book includes many of the most common puzzles and brainteasers used by Microsoft and companies in other industries. Many of the puzzles selected for this book were nominated by interviewers, recruiters, and staffing professionals who use them on a day-to-day basis. Others came from candidates themselves. For the most part, organizations are not eager to have the puzzles they use in job interviews exposed. For that reason, many of the people who have cooperated with me in assembling these puzzles have asked that their names not be used. I have respected those requests.

James Fixx, author of *Games for the Superintelligent* and other puzzle books, offers this advice for people with puzzles to solve: "One way to improve your ability to use your mind is simply to see how very bright people use theirs." The following pages detail how hundreds of very smart people have solved the puzzles and brainteasers that other very smart people have given them. In his puzzle books, Fixx valiantly tries to explain what, as he so delicately puts it, "the superintelligent do that's different from what ordinary people do."

Fixx advises people to think hard and loose and to see the problem at a slant. "The true puzzler . . . gropes for some loophole, and, with luck, quickly finds it in the third dimension." Further hints abound: "The intelligent person tries . . . not to impose unnecessary restrictions on his mind." Fixx admires determination: "The bright person has succeeded because he does not assume the problem cannot be solved simply because it cannot be solved in one way or even two ways he has tried."

Here's the paradox. The candidates whose solutions are described in this book recognize that the flashes of insight that Fixx describes, and that interviewers expect of job candidates, are more a result of intuition than rigorous logic. "What is particularly troubling is how little 'logic' seems to be involved in some phases of problem solving. Difficult problems are often solved via a sudden, intuitive insight. One moment you're stuck; the next moment this insight has popped into your head, though not by any step-by-step logic that can be recounted." But whatever it is—out-of-the-box thinking, third-eye vision—it's clear that interviewers want it.

This book is primarily intended for job seekers. You don't have time to waste, so let's get down to the question job seekers deem most important. Can this book really help me ace the brainteaser job interview? Stated another way:

Will studying help me ace the brainteaser job interview?

The answer is yes. The mind is a muscle. Creative, flexible thinking can be improved by exercise, and systematically working the logic puzzles in this book can serve as the basis for training. The strategic goal is to make creative thinking a lifelong habit. The first step is to become familiar with the norms, conventions, and traps of logic puzzles. Working the puzzles in this book can be a way to start. At a minimum, you won't be completely taken aback when you are confronted with one. Perhaps you may even be given one of the puzzles you have studied—and then you have a moral choice to make.

Perhaps the biggest benefit of working the puzzles in this book is to train your brain against betraying you when you need it the most. Most of these puzzles feature traps that exploit the laziness of our brains. Our brains make thousands of assumptions—rote assumptions—every minute just so we can get through the day. Imagine if we had to consciously analyze every action we take. Logic puzzles exploit this property of our brains by sneaking under the radar of our assumptions. Or they find wormholes in our pattern recognition.

The intelligence these puzzles seek to reveal calls on your ability to challenge rote assumptions, see patterns where they exist, and reject them where they don't. To solve these puzzles, you have to question your usual ways of thinking, brainstorm new approaches, and evaluate those new approaches critically—and those skills can be honed by simply working the puzzles in this book.

Most logic puzzles and brainteasers exploit a relatively small number of booby traps, psychological tricks, missing information, and other swindles that penalize the would-be solver. The good news is that there is often a "trick" to solving these problems. See Chapter 2 for a description of these mental tricks and shortcuts. Sometimes it's as easy as realizing that some critical information is missing. Other times it's the realization that your brain has filled in a missing piece of information—but filled it in incorrectly. If you know the trick or can quickly detect it, you will be in a much stronger position and avoid the dead ends the puzzles are designed to take you down. That in itself can give you the confidence to take the puzzle, even if you have never heard it before, to the next level.

If you want to study, a focused course in psychometrics—the study of measuring human abilities—might be helpful. A job interview is just another form of testing. Interviewers expect that the job candidates' responses to specific questions provide some useful clues about outcomes. Mostly, the responses don't, but no one has figured out a better way to select employees.

A WORD TO INTERVIEWERS AND RECRUITERS READING THIS BOOK

While this book is primarily written for job candidates, interviewers and recruiters will also find much benefit in these pages. If you currently use puzzles and brainteasers in your interviews, you will certainly increase your repertoire and perhaps find puzzles more appropriate to your staffing assignments. Even if many of these puzzles are familiar, perhaps the discussion of the solutions will increase your perspective about their implications. If you are not currently using puzzles and brainteasers, this book may introduce you to the value of adding selective puzzles to the mix of questions. The following guidelines, based on research with hundreds of recruiters and candidates, may help you get maximum benefit out of these questions and avoid some mistakes.

Try to select puzzles that have some relevance to the job and the candidates' real-world business performance. There is a correlation between specific puzzles and real-world skill sets called on by specific jobs because many of the cognitive skills needed are the same. For example, selecting candidates for a job that requires aptitude in strategic planning could be advanced by giving candidates puzzles that call on their strategic planning capacities. A search for a product manager who would be required to make a series of high-risk bets on incomplete evidence could be advanced by the use of puzzles testing quick decision-making and probability skills. The bottom line is, try to make the puzzle fit the job.

"I prefer puzzles with layers, where there isn't a 'right' answer, or maybe where there is one answer which is relatively obvious, and another which is deeper," insists Ole Eichorn, CTO of Aperio Technologies. "Good puzzles are solvable. Perhaps the biggest problem with many interview puzzles is that they're too hard. If good, smart candidates can't solve them, they aren't useful. In addition, ideal puzzles involve steady thinking and problem solving rather than an 'aha' insight," he adds.

Should you be concerned that candidates have heard puzzles before? Not really. You should expect that the best candidates have prepared for the job interview. But just because they have prepared an answer for questions such as "Tell me about a time when you solved a difficult problem?" does that mean there's no value in your asking it? By the same token, the best puzzles are the ones that depend less on a specific solution and more on reasoning. There may be one "correct" answer, but many ways of getting there. Or there may be an unlimited number of solution sets, and the fun is in exploring a handful of them. The point is to use the puzzle as the basis of a conversation. While a candidate may have memorized a puzzle and can go through the motions, a good verbal presentation is difficult to counterfeit.

PUZZLES AND BRAINTEASERS GUIDELINES FOR USE

Based on feedback from dozens of interviewers, recruiters, and staffing professionals, here are some rules and guidelines for the use of puzzles and brainteasers in job interviews:

1. *Test, test, test.* Always try out a puzzle on colleagues, friends, and the guys at the health club before using it in a job interview. Never use a candidate to test a puzzle for the first time.

2. *Know the puzzle inside and out.* Never give a puzzle that you don't thoroughly understand. Knowing the "right answer" is not enough. You need to have a deep understanding of the puzzle and every likely solution set, correct or incorrect, and you need to know how to guide the candidate through the puzzle. You are guaranteed to encounter candidates who understand the puzzle more deeply than you do. Don't embarrass yourself and the candidate.

3. *Make it win-win.* Job interview puzzles must be win-win. That is, they must not defeat the candidate. Some candidates will nail the puzzle, and others will need help. That's okay. But don't let a candidate go away feeling defeated or, worse, cheated. Let every candidate emerge feeling like a victor. Ideally, the puzzle will be a learning opportunity for both parties and, in the best cases, even fun. In other words, you need to practice having a meaningful conversation about the challenge.

4. *If in doubt, don't.* If you're not absolutely sure about a puzzle or brainteaser, don't even think about using it. Never just throw puzzles at candidates and see what sticks. Make sure you understand what information you are looking for and how you will use the results.

5. *At least one solution.* Don't ask candidates to solve a puzzle that does not have a solution. It's okay, even preferred, for puzzles to have more than one solution, but it must have at least one satisfying conclusion. Be aware of the power differential in a job interview. Asking a candidate to consider a puzzle that is impossible to solve is nothing less than a trap.

HOW THIS BOOK IS ORGANIZED

How to Ace the Brainteaser Interview organizes puzzles by category and difficulty. Starting with Chapter 3, the book deals with puzzles that, when all is said and done, have at least one preferred answer. Chapter 3—"Real-World Reasoning Puzzles"—includes puzzles that deal with concepts in physics and everyday objects. Chapter 4 has logic puzzles that do not require math more onerous than counting. Chapter 5, on the other hand, has more than two dozen logic puzzles that call on some skill in elementary arithmetic, algebra, and geometry. Chapter 6 includes some delightful puzzles that require at least some familiarity with probability theory. Chapter 7 has puzzles that are appropriate for programmers and analysts, and these puzzles require basic programming concepts for their solutions.

But many puzzles really don't have an answer, or if they do, no one cares what they are. These puzzles are about process—the steps the candidate takes to bring the puzzle to some satisfactory resolution—and these puzzles are the subject of Chapters 8 to 10. Many of these types of puzzles show up in the business case interviews favored by consulting firms. Chapter 8 lists some of the more common business cases now making the rounds. Chapter 9—"Gross Order of Estimation Problems"—features puzzles such as "How many piano tuners are there in America?" and other so-called Fermi problems. Chapter 10—"Performance Puzzles"—includes puzzles that actually require a candidate to get up and perform some activity, such as "sell me this pen."

This book presents 152 brainteasers and puzzles. Each brainteaser starts with an introduction and a statement of the puzzle. Most brainteasers include a hint that interviewers have been known to offer candidates who need a bit of help. The critical part of each puzzle is a discussion of the "aha!" opportunity as well as the booby traps and other land mines that trip up unwary candidates. The discussion of each puzzle includes advice on how to overcome these traps and provides a statement of the solution and alternative solutions, if any. To ground the book in reality as much as possible, the actual responses that interviewers deemed most outstanding are included whenever available. In some cases, the book discusses an extra credit variant of the puzzle and its solution to make you look even more perceptive.

RIDDLE ME THIS

Interviewers are looking for meaningful, uncontroversial conversations with candidates that will provide actionable information on which to make reliable selection decisions. Interviewers hope that puzzles and brainteasers will help create the possibility of such quality conversations.

Joel Spolsky, founder of Fog Creek Software and a former program manager at Microsoft, is an advocate of using brainteasers, primarily as conversation starters. "The goal is to have an interesting conversation with the candidate, and to use that conversation to see how smart and capable they are," Spolsky explains. "If you have an interesting conversation about certain types of topics with a person, you can determine if [he] is the type of person you want to hire. The questions are almost a pretext to having that conversation."

In almost all cases, the interviewers are less interested in the answer you offer than in the road you use getting there. It's all about process. To that extent, the best strategy is to take your time, think out loud, and let the interviewer see you sweat (at least a little). Ironically, solving these puzzles too fast may work against you. At a minimum, the interviewer may conclude you've heard the puzzle before. In any case, even if you impress the interviewer with your speed, you will have missed the opportunity to talk about how you would use the skills you just demonstrated to add value to the company. Let the interviewer participate with you in solving the puzzle.

The truth is, puzzles generally make up less than 10 percent of any job interview. "The puzzles are a small part of the interview process at Microsoft," says Ron Jacobs, product manager for the Platform Architecture Guidance Team. "We've found it's very effective in giving us insight into a candidate's potential. And that potential is the hardest thing to gauge. We know the résumé looks good, and they seem to have the skills. These puzzles put them in a place where it's just them and their raw thinking abilities."

Jacobs says that the puzzles are usually designed so that there are no clear answers. Sometimes the interviewer will throw a candidate a hint that points to a solution that is clearly wrong, just to see how the candidate will defend his or her position and push back. "A level of confidence is good," Jacobs says. "Microsoft is very much a company that values that kind of independent thought." But don't let the attitude slip into stubbornness or arrogance, he adds.

Jacobs speaks from experience. He should know, because he's had three interviews at Microsoft. In 1997, in his first time at bat, Jacobs impressed people that he was a "Microsoft hire," but he was nevertheless thought not a good fit for the position at hand. In his first interview, he was asked to design an airport. Jacobs immediately began to wax eloquent about how he would design a world-class international airport like Seattle's SeaTac or Chicago's O'Hare. But after letting Jacobs go on for five minutes, the interviewer stopped him and said, "But all I need is a small regional airport." Jacobs learned a lesson: "I didn't clarify precisely what the customer needed."

In his second interview a year later, Jacobs anticipated brainteasers but didn't get any. He was asked to solve a coding problem instead. Since then, he's interviewed for an internal job. "My take on the big picture here is that when we ask these questions we are looking not so much for the answer, but how the candidate thinks about the problem and approaches the solution," Jacobs notes. "Some candidates will be very quiet for a few minutes and then spew out an answer. This is generally a bad approach," he says. "A better approach is for candidates to think out loud as though they were collaborating with me on the answer. I especially like to hear them ask questions which clarify the problem. Sometimes we will ask an intentionally vague question to test for this."

THE INTERVIEWER'S DILEMMA

Selectivity is the key reason for interviewers including puzzles in the mix. Interviewers believe that puzzles help them separate the outstanding candidates from the great ones. Ironically, a recession that creates a seller's market (more candidates applying for each job) only aggravates the interviewer's dilemma. Selectivity becomes harder, not easier, when dozens or even hundreds of candidates chase each position. Now interviewers are confronted with an abundance of outstanding candidates who all seem perfectly suited to the requirements of the job. Each has passed the preemployment background screening and sports a sterling résumé, the requisite technical skills, the appropriate certifications. Pastures of plenty! It's easy to distinguish between an average performer and a superstar. But what do you do when you have to select among superstars?

You may have noticed that the job reference, once the backbone of any recruitment process, is nowhere mentioned. Over the past 25 years, organizations have become increasingly reluctant to provide references for former employees. The reluctance is not hard to understand. In our litigious society, job applicants—whether downsized or voluntarily separated— have their attorney's telephone number on speed dial, ready to push the button for any perceived slight. As a result, most organizations will limit reference checks to verifying dates of employment and job title and final salary at separation. An increasing number of companies automate the reference-checking process using touch-tone voice-response systems to eliminate the chance that a human might say something that a former employee can claim was defamatory.

Letters of reference, once key to the hiring process, are likewise obsolete. Even on the rare occasions when they are submitted, reference-letter inflation makes them less useful. Every reference is glowing; every applicant is flawless. If they were so flawless, interviewers rightly wonder, why are they unemployed? No one wants to take the risk of writing a letter that is nuanced. Besides, with many candidates applying through the Internet, there's often no opportunity to submit letters or attachments of any kind.

Today, even the traditional job interview—the most valuable tool in deciding on the "fit" of a potential employee—is circumscribed. Interviewers are running scared. Interviewers now have to worry about subjects they need to *avoid* and questions they are *not* allowed to ask. In the United States, state and federal law take a whole swath of topics and questions off the table. Interviewers are not supposed to ask a candidate's age, weight, marital status, ethnicity, national origin, citizenship, political outlook, sexual preference, financial status, or reproductive plans. Except for specific jobs, interviewers can't even ask about a candidate's arrest record. Only questions that point to the candidate's ability to do the job at hand are allowed. Many of these rules protect women and minorities, and that's good. No one wants to go back to the days when employers asked women job applicants about their birth control practices. But the new rules also create uncertainty about the kind of small talk that is vital for any human interaction. Innocent questions such as, "Did you have trouble getting here?" become ominous when the interviewer is afraid that the candidate may wonder if the question is just an icebreaker or an attempt to discover if the candidate drove or took the bus.

For these reasons and more, puzzles and brainteasers are making a comeback. Employers are desperate. It's all part of an increasing emphasis to use the job interview to provide actionable information on which to make reliable judgments. With many job interview questions off the table, puzzles and brainteasers become more attractive as a way to have extended conversations with candidates. By asking candidates to respond to a puzzle or brainteaser, the conversations not only stay on safe ground, but create an opportunity to have a conversation that genuinely reveals critical aspects of how the candidate approaches a challenge, formulates a response, and articulates a strategy. When most of the candidates on the short list are overqualified for the position, these types of conversations, interviewers hope, can give them a meaningful basis on which to make a selection.

PUZZLES THAT WORK

Puzzles appropriate for job interviews help catalyze a meaningful conversation between the candidate and the interviewer. It is in this conversation, more than the solution to any particular puzzle, that the value of the interview is experienced.

The world is full of puzzles, but relatively few of them are appropriate for job interviews. Most, for one reason or another, simply don't create extended conversations (see Appendix D for types of puzzles inappropriate for job interviews). The puzzles that have the best possible traction for interviews have these attributes:

4

- *Have solutions.* Puzzles are meant to be solved.

- *Short.* The puzzle statement is clean, crisp, and obvious. Puzzles with elaborate narrations or many conditions don't work well. The best puzzles can be solved in less than five minutes, although the conversations about them can be extended.

- *Open ended.* Puzzles that have multiple acceptable answers allow candidates to be creative or demonstrate their ability to come up with multiple solutions. Most of all, if there are no right or wrong answers, candidates cannot be defeated.

- *Unobvious.* By this, I mean not only that the problem is "deep" in some nontrivial way, but that it often suggests an "obvious" first impression that is inevitably wrong.

- *Charming.* The best puzzles engage our intellects in ways that leave candidates stimulated. It's hard to define what gives a puzzle this quality, but we know it when we see it. Puzzles shouldn't be arduous. One goal of puzzles in job interviews is to have fun while doing serious business.

STRATEGIES FOR SOLUTIONS

Employers who ask puzzles in interviews are often looking for people who are good at divergent reasoning. Divergent reasoning, as opposed to convergent reasoning, is the process of finding previously undiscovered solutions to problems.

The tools you need to solve problems with divergent thinking are originality, adaptability, fluency, and inventiveness. Divergent thinkers examine all assumptions, stated and especially unstated. The typical divergent thinker will usually explore many possible solutions before finding the optimum one.

Convergent reasoning is likely to pick the first reasonable solution that presents itself. It is often based on an unaware acceptance of unstated assumptions. And once having articulated a solution, convergent thinkers tend to stick with that one alternative, defending it like a dog with a chew bone. The minds of convergent thinkers are trapped on one-way streets. Henry Ford's famous slogan about model T Fords—"You can have any color you desire so long as it's black"—is a classic example of convergent thinking. And while there are occasions where convergent thinking is desirable, the job interview is assuredly not one of them.

LET THE FORCE BE WITH YOU

By "the Force," I mean the conventions of puzzles and brainteasers. Puzzle solvers have evolved a set of agreements about how puzzles behave. It's a world inhabited by characters that look like people but often act in ways that would in the real world appear totally goofy.

For example, there are a group of games called balance puzzles. In these puzzles, the challenge is to find among a group the one thing that weighs more or less than the others using the smallest number of weighings. Fair enough. Let's say it's a coin. In the real world, you might do all kinds of things with the coin. You might saw it in half, melt it down, grind it into powder, chew on it, heft it in your hands, do a chemical analysis, look on the Internet, bribe a jeweler, etc. Some of these strategies may be inspired; others may be stupid; none of them have a place in a balance puzzle. Puzzle conventions won't tolerate such distractions. So get into the spirit of this world. Embrace the constraints as offered and attend to the abstracted geometry of the challenge.

When puzzles are animated by humanlike creatures, it's important to forget practically everything you know about complex, ambivalent human behavior. Puzzle creatures are simple, one-dimensional characters who exist only to serve the puzzle. They usually have but one motivation. Depending on the puzzle, these characters are concerned only with maximizing money, escaping the fire, moving items across a bridge, or behaving in predictable ways. Puzzle creatures understand probability, and when they are expected to act logically, they never fail. These creatures act instantaneously and are thoroughly aware of the logical consequences of their actions. Puzzle creatures never make mistakes, nor are they ever uncertain. Puzzle creatures don't have an altruistic bone in their bodies; they never do anything because they are nice or it's the fair thing to do. When they act, it's for their self-interest alone.

Even brilliant people can crumple under the pressure of a job interview. But don't despair. Here are a few practical tips to make the task easier. Heed what dozens of interviewers, recruiters, and job coaches have to say about confronting puzzles and brainteasers.

- *The obvious answer is always wrong.* Depend on it—your first thought is undependable. The more obvious the answer seems, the more incorrect it is likely to be. Almost all puzzles are deeper than they appear to be—that's what makes them puzzles. By all means, note the obvious answer. Even share it with the interviewer, but always with a measure of suspicion. Now take the obvious answer and consider why it's wrong.

- *Work the answer, not the question.* All the information you need is already there. Nothing is missing.

- *Think first, and then speak.* Don't be afraid of silence. Take a minute or even two to think about the problem. "We want you to think, so think," a Microsoft interviewer observes. Look like you think about every answer. Paradoxically, most interviewers reward deliberation more than speed, so even if you think you know the answer before the interviewer is finished with the puzzle, appear to think about it. Your first thought may be wrong. And never interrupt the interviewer.

- *Break it down.* Smaller is more manageable. If the puzzle involves five marbles, see what would happen with two marbles.

- *Back-translate.* Repeat what you have just heard. State the goal of the problem. You do this for several reasons: First, you get to hear the case all over again. Second, you show the interviewer that you were listening. And third, you do not end up answering the wrong question, which happens more often than you would think.

- *A dialogue is better than a monologue.* Be transparent. Think out loud. Let the interviewer see you struggle with the problem. Show the logic path your mind is taking. An interview is often structured like an exam, but a lot of answers can be worth partial credit. If you're talking out loud, an interviewer knows where you are and can give you hints.

- *Honor Occam's razor.* Favor the economical solution. Occam's razor is the proposition that when two explanations account for a situation, the simpler explanation is better. In the case of job interview puzzles, you can be pretty sure that the puzzles are less complicated than the solutions you are considering. Keep it simple.

- *We're having fun, aren't we?* Use inclusive language—*we* and *our*—as you solve the problem. Inclusive language indicates your preference for teamwork and collaboration. If you do it right, it gives the impression that you are already part of the team.

- *Ask questions; don't just give answers.* Sometimes this means challenging the puzzle, but mostly it means asking clarifying questions. Make sure you are answering the problem being asked. Use questions to establish the scope of the problem before digging deep in one area.

- *Calculus is never required.* If you find yourself working a calculus problem, stop immediately. These puzzles never require more than simple arithmetic. In general, the more complicated the question, the simpler the answer.

- *Work backward.* Often the solution is easier when you start from the end of the puzzle and work backward.

- *All things being equal, give the interviewer a unique answer.* A good way to stand out is to give the interviewer a solution he or she has never heard before.

- *Go for closure.* Often you will drift back and forth between two or more equally attractive solutions. You must pick and commit yourself. You don't have to have a good reason, except for the need to move on. That's just good business, and interviewers will respect you for it.

- *Ask for the answer.* If you don't get the answer or the interviewer indicates he or she has another answer in mind, ask for it. Never fail to turn the conversation into a learning opportunity.

HELP! I'M TOTALLY STUMPED

The human brain is a marvelous organ. It starts working the minute you are born and doesn't stop until you are hit with one of these logic puzzles. When that happens, don't worry. The way you handle a puzzle you can't solve is almost as important as the way you handle a puzzle you can.

The biggest mistake is to get all flummoxed and react like a deer in headlights—too stunned to respond or survive. Worse is to act like a drowning swimmer, lash out at the interviewer, and take him or her down with you. A good response does not always mean coming up with the right answer, but it does mean showing good approaches to an unfamiliar problem.

The best thing is to keep your sense of humor. One very people-smart candidate responded to a very difficult puzzle this way: "Hmmm . . . one of us doesn't know the answer." Another, referring to the popular TV quiz show *Who Wants to Be a Millionaire?* in which contestants get to make one phone call for help, asked: "How many lifelines do I have?"

When you feel stuck, the first thing to do is to take a deep breath and ask for the puzzle to be repeated. Now listen. Sometimes the interviewer will sense something and provide a missing emphasis or detail. Then repeat the puzzle to the interviewer. "Let me see if I have this right . . ." Then repeat it again. Sometimes saying a puzzle aloud to yourself once or twice reveals some opportunity for taking it to the next level. Some candidates take time to write the problem down. Don't let yourself be rushed.

Then ask questions. If there's a detail you don't understand, let the interviewer know. Own the difficulty. "I'm having trouble with this problem. Can you help me understand . . .?" If none of this helps, ask for a hint. "I'm sorry. I seem to be stuck. Can you give me a hint?"

Don't let interviewers see you panic, but let them see you think out loud. "You have to show them that your mind is cycling," says former Microsoft developer Adam Barr. "Have your internal dialogue out loud. Show them that you're curious. Let them see the answers you explore and the dead ends you're considering; invite them to go with you down the blind alleys. Even if you never get right to the answer, they might be impressed by your strategy."

Finally, if you really are at a dead end and have nowhere to go, just admit that you'll need more time than you feel comfortable taking in a job interview. Don't admit you can't do the problem; just suggest you can't do it in the time frame of the interview. Barr suggests wording like, "I'm sorry. I can't work out the problem right here, but given time I'm sure I can do it. May I get back to you?" Even if you don't get it, make sure the interviewer sees your curiosity and unflagging spirit. "I know I didn't get it, but I'm really curious. Can you tell me what the solution is?" This kind of closure replaces the sting of failure with a sense of optimism about the next puzzle.

Some candidates feel insulted by puzzles and brainteasers and treat them like "illegal" questions. Some simply say, "My policy is not to respond to questions like that." Others respond with a challenge of their own. "What does that puzzle have to do with my ability to perform on this job?" Most interviewers will respect your position. They won't hire you, but they will respect your position. If it's respect you want, then by all means pursue this course. If it's a job offer you want, then accept that for a candidate to engage in conflict on a job interview is counter-productive. You may not like puzzles—you may find them insulting—but if you want to be considered for the job, there's no alternative but to take your best shot.

11

REAL-WORLD REASONING PUZZLES

Sometimes the most common artifacts of our lives are the most puzzling. How well do candidates observe the world in which they live? How curious are they about the phenomena, both natural and artificial, that fill the corners of our daily lives? How easily can they manipulate the tools and concepts that allow people to display the kind of intelligence people still call "common sense"? These puzzles test all kinds of skills— curiosity, observation, pattern recognition, for example—useful in business. Interviewers believe that asking candidates puzzles like the ones in this chapter provide a glimpse into how candidates engage the world around them. And it's a bonus that many of these problems are just plain fun.

1 MANHOLE COVERS

"Why are manhole covers round?" This is the mother of all job interview brainteasers. Actually, the puzzle should be more precisely phrased as *"why are manhole covers circular?"* This is the puzzle that may have started the recent trend of routinely using brainteasers in job interviews. One of the founding myths of Microsoft is that CEO Steve Ballmer was jogging with another Microsoft executive when he stepped on a manhole cover. It was round, and it occurred to him that every manhole cover he had ever seen had a similar shape. *"Why are manhole covers round?"* Ballmer asked himself. Within a few hundred yards, Ballmer had worked out three reasons. *"Hmmm, that would be a good question to ask in interviews."*

Why are manhole covers circular?

For years in the early 1980s, job candidates coming for their job interviews would yell upon arriving on the Microsoft campus, "Because they won't fall into the hole!" And the puzzle still shows up because it's a classic. Interviewers get good clues about the candidate even if he or she has studied the classic responses. Here are the classic responses, in order of their popularity:

1. Circular covers are the only geometric shape that won't fall into the manhole shaft they cover.
2. Circular manhole covers don't need to be aligned or oriented with the manhole shaft.
3. Circular manhole covers make it easier to lift, carry, or even roll the heavy items.
4. The manufacture of circular manhole covers is cheaper because it requires less metal than the manufacture of covers of any other shape.
5. Because manholes are circular!

The puzzle really extends beyond just picking an answer. A candidate is expected to pick one or two responses and then defend them. A Microsoft recruiter found the following response perfectly reasonable for its grounding in moral values. It's always good to remind the interviewer that these real-world problems are focused on preserving human safety:

> A circular cover is the only geometric shape that won't fall into the hole and possibly injure someone below or create a hazard for someone above. The slight lip on the manhole cover shaft prevents the cover from ever falling in, no matter how it's held. A square manhole cover just wouldn't work as well. That's because the diagonal of a square is the square root of 2 times its side. Should a square manhole cover be held near-vertically and turned just a little, it would fall easily into the shaft. The same is true with triangular shapes. Circular shapes alone, because a circle has the same diameter in all directions, have the property we are looking for.

If you want to go with another response, fine. All these responses can work, so pick one and be prepared for the objections and conversation. This puzzle is not about your engineering skills. It's about evaluating your ability to make a decision, communicate your reasoning, and defend it.

Avoid the temptation to be a smart aleck. Yes, there are other shapes besides circular that satisfy the condition that the cover be unable to fall into the shaft. But bringing the class of shapes referred to as Reuleaux polygons into the conversation will not advance your chances unless you're applying for a topology position.

Extra credit: The reality is that not all manhole covers are circular. Dan Heller is a photographer who maintains a Web page of dozens of photos of manhole covers (many with his shoes visible in the photo) that he takes on his assignments around the world (http://www.danheller.com/manholes.html). While most of the manhole covers are indeed circular, clearly some municipalities prefer square and rectangular covers.

2 ELIMINATE A STATE

This is one of the most popular questions still asked at Microsoft. I've talked to dozens of people who have been asked this question. In each case the interviewer seems to have a different "correct" answer in mind.

If you had to eliminate one of the 50 U.S. states, which one would you select? Be prepared to give specific reasons why you chose the state you did.

Don't get hung up looking for a "correct" answer." There is no correct answer, unless you're applying for a job with Microsoft, in which case Washington State is definitely a nonstarter. The best course is to reframe the question in some compelling way. Another idea: Don't start with the name of a state, but build some suspense by walking the interviewer through your logic and seeing where you end up together. Humor always helps. There are dozens of creative answers. Here are three of them.

1. Well, I don't want to be responsible for eliminating actual people. So I'd eliminate the political entity of a state by ceding it to

Canada, perhaps a state that shares a border with Canada, such as North Dakota or Vermont. Would I still be able to visit?

2. A similar approach calls for eliminating a state by actually combining it with one of its neighbors. For example, Connecticut can annex Rhode Island. Or North and South Dakota can be combined to form the state of Dakota.

3. I'd eliminate Wyoming [you get points for knowing that Wyoming is the least populous state], but only if the people and natural attributes can be relocated to a theme park on the Las Vegas strip.

Candidates should be aware that some interviewers have an agenda when asking this question and want candidates to come to a certain conclusion. One candidate reports that when he was asked this question, the interviewer indicated the "correct" answer was to divide a square state (like Colorado or Wyoming) into several parts (presumably rectangular) and merge them with the neighbor states. It turns out that the interviewer had Colorado in mind as the ideal response. Listen to how angry the candidate was:

I thought I had covered every realistic possibility, but it boiled down to the interviewer being totally arbitrary. At the end, it was more like "but what about splitting a state into multiple regions and combining with all the neighbors" and "Colorado is rectangular and easy to divide" and so forth. She had no comment either way about my other solutions and was totally stuck on dividing Colorado. I wasn't sure if she wanted me to go into depth about satellite photography and how it isn't that tough with modern technology to divide an irregularly shaped state into equal parts, or admit that dividing a state into multiple parts is a valid method that I skipped. She was very hung up on dividing equally area wise, as if population densities or other considerations didn't matter. We talked for a long time, as a portion of the interview, about why I thought involving more states made it less likely for success, and she always seemed to ignore this reasoning and return to dividing Colorado equally. So maybe the interviewer had some grudge against the state of Colorado, was fascinated with that state's rectangular shape or fascinated with easy geometric constructions (divide a rectangle into equal areas). Or was just being difficult for the sake of being difficult.

Of course, the interviewer might have been testing how the candidate reacted if she pushed back on the candidate's solution.

3 A QUESTION OF BALANCE

This may seem like a trivial question, but Ed Milano, vice president of marketing and program development at Design Continuum (www.dcontinuum.com), a product design consulting firm with offices in Boston, Milan, and Seoul, finds it can be revealing.

There are two people who want to balance on a seesaw. The first person weighs 125 pounds. The second person weighs 150 pounds. How do they have to arrange themselves so the seesaw is balanced horizontally? (See Figure 3.1.)

For Milano to make a job offer, he has to see how the candidate thinks under stressful conditions, the environment that often describes life at a consultancy that assists clients with make-or-break strategic design programs. "We never solve the same problem twice; every engagement is unique," Milano says. "So we're looking for people who think about new things in a new way, eager to move past established limits, and are confident enough to push their teammates over their respective boundaries."

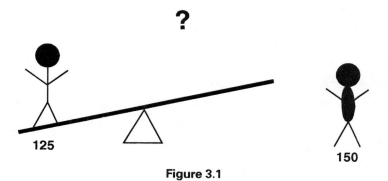

Figure 3.1

17

What kind of response is Milano looking for? "At a minimum, the candidate needs to communicate that the heavier person must sit closer to the pivot point than the lighter person. If the candidate gets up to draw the configuration on the whiteboard, I see evidence that the candidate conceptualizes in images," he says. For a designer, that's good.

For a more elaborate seesaw puzzle, see puzzle 93.

Solution: The heavier person must sit closer to the fulcrum.

4 SALT AND PEPPER

This is a charming puzzle reminiscent of junior high school physics experiments. Some recruiters like to use it during lunch interviews.

Imagine that we sprinkle some salt on a piece of white paper. Then we sprinkle some pepper over the salt. Now, using only a plastic comb, how would you separate the salt from the pepper?

Hint: The answer will shock you.

Pull the comb through your hair several times. This will create static electricity and attach a negative charge to the comb. Now wave the comb over the salt-pepper combination and the pepper, being much lighter, will attach itself to the comb. The salt crystals, being much heavier, will be left behind.

5 ROPE LADDER, RISING TIDE

This puzzle is almost too much of a trick question, but some interviewers find it a good way to start an interview. Here, the interviewer is looking for a candidate who can "picture" a problem and thereby find the solution obvious.

A rope ladder hangs over the side of a ship. The rungs are 1 foot apart, and the ladder is 12 feet long. The tide is rising at 4 inches an hour. How long will it take before the first four rungs of the ladder are under water?

Hint: Buoyancy.

Candidates must be wary of problems that sound too easy. There's always a trap. No interviewer would offer a problem that requires such trivial math, so the issue becomes a meta-problem: what's the unstated puzzle? In this case, the real puzzle is to realize that the frame of reference is inclusive. The ship and the rope ladder act as a unit. The rope ladder, being attached to the ship, rises with the rising water, and if it is not submerged now, it will never be submerged no matter how high the water rises.

Solution: Forever.

6 COCONUTS

This is also a trick question, but its solution calls for a mind that is flexible in its scaling and unbound by a deep-seated assumption that trips up almost everyone confronting this puzzle. There's a cute preferred answer, but the resulting conversation can go in any number of interesting places. That's what a good puzzle is intended to do.

A businessman devises a business plan for buying and selling coconuts. He calculates that by buying coconuts for $5 a dozen and selling them for $3 a dozen, that in less than a year he will be a millionaire. His business plan and calculations are accurate. How is this possible?

Hint: *Starting conditions.*

When we hear puzzles like this, most of us start thinking in dot-com terms: elaborate rationalizations of why losing money is a sound business proposition. Some candidates respond by suggesting the businessman is building market share by giving away product at below cost. Or that his strategy is to drive his competitor out of business so that he can then control the coconut market. All well and good, but these responses always assume a starting condition that the businessman has more money at the end of the experiment than before. Perhaps the most elegant answer is to conclude that the guy is perpetually going to lose money with this scheme, so that if he ends up a millionaire, he had to have started out as a billionaire.

Solution: The businessman started out as a billionaire.

7 HOLE IN THE IRON WASHER

This is a good warm-up question for a job interview. Some candidates shoot themselves in the foot by making the question more complicated than it is. There's something about the concept of holes that confuses people.

What happens to the hole in an iron washer when the washer is heated? Does the size of the hole decrease, increase, or stay the same?

Hint: What happens when metal is heated?

When a piece of metal is heated or cooled, it expands or contracts uniformly. The effect is just the same as if the whole thing were scaled up or scaled down. The iron washer would expand when heated, as would the hole in it.

Solution: The hole gets larger.

8 SIX WATER GLASSES

Another puzzle for interviewers who like puzzles that involve manipulatables. It can be presented using Figure 3.2 or using actual glasses of water or, as in this example, orange juice.

Here are six glasses. Three of these glasses contain orange juice (or water). Moving only one glass, can you arrange the glasses such that those containing the orange juice (or water) are next to each together, without any empty glasses in between?

Hint: Pouring is moving.

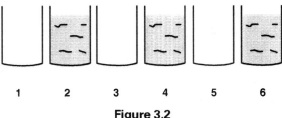

Figure 3.2

Solution: Pick up glass 2 (from left to right) and empty its contents into the empty glass 5.

9 EAST COAST, WEST COAST

This puzzle has a satisfying solution, but should be restricted to candidates who are expected to be familiar with the geography of the United States and the fact that East Coast and West Coast states are separated by two time zones—Central and Mountain Time—and when it is noon in, say, New York, it is 9 a.m. in, say, California.

Two people are talking long distance on the phone; one is physically in an East Coast state of the United States, the other is in a West Coast state of the United States. That is, the East Coast state borders the Atlantic Ocean; the West Coast state borders the Pacific Ocean. The first person asks the other, "What time is it?" When he hears the answer, he says, "That's funny. I'm only one hour earlier than you." How is that possible?

Hint: East is East and West is West and never the twain shall meet. But they come closer than you think.

As far as I can tell, there's only one reasonable solution to this puzzle. One of the people is in eastern Oregon (a West Coast state that borders the Pacific, yet whose eastern portion is in Mountain Time). The other person is in western Florida (an East Coast state that borders the Atlantic, yet whose western portion is in Central Time). The difference between Mountain and Central Time is one hour.

Solution: One person is in eastern Oregon; the other is in western Florida.

Extra credit: The puzzle can be made even more challenging by making the time for each person the same. This is possible if it happens to be at the exact moment when daylight savings changes at 2:00 a.m.

10 HEADS-UP COINS

To some people, this puzzle is trivial; to others, its solution is hard to fathom even after it is explained. Most interviewers prefer to present this puzzle as an abstract word problem, but it can also be presented with coins or playing cards. The blindfolding is definitely not recommended.

You are blindfolded and are presented with a collection of coins on a table. You are told that exactly 26 coins show heads. How can you divide all the coins into two sets, with the same number of coins showing heads in each set? You cannot distinguish, by sight or by touch, which coins are showing heads or tails.

Hint: The two piles don't have to have the same number of coins.

Solution: Select 26 coins at random to be one pile (or in general, select a number equal to the number of coins specified showing heads), and simply turn the coins in that pile over. Call all remaining coins the second pile. The two piles now have the same number of coins showing heads. Many people doubt that the solution is this simple. One candidate explained it this way:

> Let's assume there are 50 coins in total. We know only 26 coins of the 50 show heads. Now, the first pile will have 26 coins; the second pile will have 24 coins. Let's assume that, by pure chance, the 26 coins I selected are all showing heads. When I reverse the pile, there will be zero coins showing heads in either pile. Take another case. Assume that the first pile includes 26 coins of which 10 coins show heads and 16 coins show tails. By reversing the first pile, I end up with 10 coins showing tails and 16 coins showing heads. In this case, the other pile of 24 coins has 16 coins showing heads plus 8 coins showing tails. Both piles have 16 coins showing heads.

11 HOTEL HOT WATER

Most businesspeople are well acquainted with hotels for which this question is true. One recruiter often uses this question this way: He starts by asking, "Is your hotel comfortable?" The candidate will generally say yes, and then the interviewer says . . .

Why is it that, when you turn on the hot water in most hotels, you don't have to wait for the water to warm up like you do at home? That is, why is the water that comes out of the faucet instantly hot?

Hint: Recirculate the question.

The interviewer really doesn't care if you know the engineering that makes this little miracle possible. Rather, the interviewer is looking for you to make analogies, brainstorm, reach for metaphors, and articulate a reasonable conclusion. The answer doesn't have to be technically correct, just reasonable or reasonably creative. One candidate responded:

> Let's see. In my apartment building, I have to let the hot water run a few minutes before it gets warm. That's because the water heater is a long way from the hot-water taps and the water in the pipes cools down when no water is flowing. Let me brainstorm a couple of reasons why hot-water faucets in hotels instantly dispense hot water. One is that the pipes are heated. Another is that each bathroom has an on-demand water heater.

By this point, most interviewers would be quite satisfied and ready to move on. These responses are totally acceptable even though they happen to be wrong. No matter. Unless you are applying for a job in hotel plant maintenance, the interviewer doesn't care. The candidate has demonstrated a fluency of thinking, creative responses grounded in an understanding of elementary physics, and the capacity to analogize new solutions from familiar experiences. One word of caution: If you tell the interviewer that you are going to brainstorm, do so and avoid evaluating the suggestions.

If you knew or could reason out the correct answer, so much the better. Here's the real reason: Hotels feature a hot-water recirculating system. This system consists of a pump attached to an extra water line that connects the farthest hot-water tap directly to the hot-water heater. The pump slowly circulates hot water through the hot-water lines so that there is never standing water that cools down. Thus when you turn on the hot water, the line water is already warmed up.

Solution: Hotels exploit a hot-water recirculating system.

12 CAR BALLOONS

Everyone can easily imagine this puzzle as a thought experiment. Yet almost everyone gets it wrong. The trick here is to realize that the behavior of gases is not always the same as the behavior of solids.

You are in a stopped car with a helium balloon floating in the passenger compartment. All the windows are closed. The car accelerates forward. With respect to the passenger compartment, does the balloon move forward, move backward, or stay stationary?

Hint: *The air moves, too.*

The obvious answer is that the balloon has a tendency to move backward in the passenger compartment, as do all the CDs on the dashboard. In fact, the balloon will move forward in the passenger compartment because inertia forces the air molecules back, creating low pressure up front into which the balloon moves. Try it.

Solution: The balloon will move forward.

13 BEER ACROSS THE BORDER

This is almost a cross between a logic puzzle and a business case. It calls for an understanding of the value created by commercial transactions.

Consider a point in time when the Canadian and U.S. dollars are discounted by 10 cents on each side of the border (i.e., a Canadian dollar is worth 90 U.S. cents in the United States, and a U.S. dollar is worth 90 Canadian cents in Canada). A man walks into a bar on the U.S. side of the border, orders 10 U.S. cents' worth of beer, pays with a U.S. dollar, and receives a Canadian dollar in change. He then walks across the border to Canada, orders 10 Canadian cents' worth of beer, pays with a Canadian dollar, and receives a U.S. dollar in change. He continues going back and forth across the border buying beer

and at the end of the day ends up dead drunk with the original dollar in his pocket. The question is, Who pays for all the beer the man drinks?

Hint: What value or work does the man provide?

The first task is to decide if any economic work has been accomplished? In fact, there has. As he transported Canadian dollars into Canada and U.S. dollars into the United States, the man performed "economic work" by moving currency to a location where it was in greater demand (and thus valued higher). The earnings from this work were spent on the drinks.

Solution: The simplest answer is that the man pays for all the beer he consumes. So how does he end up with the same amount of money? Because he did economic work for which he received payment in the form of beer. A more economically technical answer is that the beer was paid for by whoever was holding the dollars when they were devalued from $1.00 to $.90. If the bills are devalued by crossing the border, then the above answer is certainly correct. But this second, more general formulation also covers the case where the dollars were simply devalued suddenly, creating a loss for each person holding the "wrong" country's dollar. For example, a U.S. citizen with U.S. $1 in his pocket can buy 10 beers in the United States. If he crosses the border, where the money is discounted by 10 percent, he suddenly can buy only 9 beers. For each dollar he takes across the border, he loses a beer. When the man takes that dollar back to its country of origin, he is drinking the beer that citizen lost.

Extra credit: Note that the man can continue to do this "work" only until the Canadian bar runs out of U.S. dollars or the United States bar runs out of Canadian dollars. At that point, he runs out of "work" to do.

14 REVERSING MIRRORS

This is a puzzle favorite at Microsoft, and so it is included here, although I don't recommend using it except in the most specific circumstances. It is infernally slippery to discuss, and some very specific language is required if there is to be a deep discussion of the physics involved. Few interviewers have the understanding or patience that this puzzle requires.

There are more direct puzzles that test the deep insights this puzzle is supposed to expose.

Why do mirrors reverse right and left but not up and down?

Hint: Challenge the assumption. Mirrors may not really reverse right and left after all.

This puzzle continues to totally flummox some very bright people, some of whom have actually studied the question. That's because a mirror is an everyday object we think we understand. Actually, most of us don't. Another problem is that this brainteaser is in a class by itself. You can't solve it with ordinary math. Not even logic can dent it. A solution even evades common sense. It requires the candidate to let go of all assumptions, and that's what makes the puzzle so revealing. The interviewer wants to see how you react to a puzzle that really throws you.

There are some very ingenious wrong answers. Here is, perhaps, the most creative: "The mirror does reverse top to bottom, but our brains recognize that the shape should be right-side-up, and flips it for us." Very smart, but why don't our brains also "correct" left to right reversing?

The critical insight to solving the reflection problem is to realize that the statement of the problem leads to hopeless confusion. Some candidates never recover because they try to answer the question as stated. Besides, normal language doesn't provide the tools to properly analyze this question. The best response may be to challenge the statement of the question: A mirror doesn't necessarily reverse left and right *or* up and down. The puzzle really tests a willingness to reflect independent thinking, even to the point of challenging assumptions posed by the interviewer. One candidate responded to the mirror puzzle like this:

> I don't think the problem is stated quite right. Mirrors don't reverse left and right; they reverse front and back. Stated another way, mirrors invert front to back, not left to right. An easy way to prove this is to stand facing north with a mirror in front of you. Wave your left (west) hand. The image in the mirror waves its west hand too, so there is no left-right reversal. The popular misconception of the inversion is caused by the fact that when person A looks at another person B,

person A expects person B to face him or her. But when person A faces himself (in the mirror), he sees an uninverted person A.

Books have been written about this subject. Resist the temptation to summarize their points.

Extra credit: But if you have to quote someone, quote from Martin Gardner, the patron saint of mathematical diversions. Here's Gardner's take on the mirror puzzle: "Human beings are superficially and grossly bilaterally symmetrical, but subjectively and behaviorally they are relatively asymmetrical. The very fact that we can distinguish our right from our left side implies an asymmetry of the perceiving system. We are thus, to a certain extent, an asymmetrical mind dwelling in a bilaterally symmetrical body, at least with respect to a casual visual inspection of our external form." (From *Hexaflexagons and Other Mathematical Diversions*, University of Chicago Press, 1988, page 170.) On second thought, don't.

15 SHOWER CURTAIN

Almost all people have experienced this experiment. How observant are they? And if they haven't really paid attention, can they reason out the physics to find a solution?

When you turn on the water spray in a shower stall with a shower curtain, which way does the bottom of the shower curtain move? Does the bottom of the shower curtain get pushed out of the stall, remain stationary, or get pulled into the stall? Assume that the shower curtain is hanging without friction and that the water spray does not directly hit the curtain.

The obvious solution (wrong, naturally) is that the spray of the water pushes air out of the shower stall, forcing the shower curtain to be pushed out. If that happens, it's because the pressure of the water is directly moving the curtain. When the water does not hit the shower curtain, air is pushed out of the shower stall, but the air escapes from the top of the enclosure (especially if it is a hot shower). The resulting low pressure at the bottom of the shower stall forces air in, the movement of which flutters the shower curtain toward the enclosure. A candidate who was posed this question, and failed to answer it correctly—and wasn't offered the job—says he will never take another shower without being reminded of this job interview.

Solution: The shower curtain is pulled into the shower stall.

16 CAR KEY TURNING

This favorite puzzler at Microsoft is less about eliciting one answer or another, but rather about getting you to give a well-considered reason for your answer. Despite the wording of the problem, the number of possible reasons for which way to turn a car key is more than a binary solution. In fact, the domain of possible reasons is the real solution space for the puzzle. On the other hand, the increasing popularity of the remote locking system makes the puzzle much less immediate.

Which way should the key turn in a car door to unlock it? Clockwise or counterclockwise?

Hint: What's the predominant handedness of people?

Reportedly, this vintage puzzle still pops up from time to time at Microsoft. That's because it is so Zenlike. Right or left. Most interviewers say the answer really doesn't matter as long as candidates defend their decision. What they are looking for are candidates who can make an essentially arbitrary decision and defend it without getting hung up about it. This puzzle actually tests a viable skill, since most of the business decisions we are called on to defend are equally arbitrary.

For some reason no one has been able to fathom, the question never asks in what direction the key should turn to *lock* the car. It's always to unlock it. But there may be a clue in this (see extra credit).

If the distribution of right- and left-handed people in the world were equal, it probably really wouldn't matter. But since most people are right-handed, a good case can be made for designing car locks to unlock by turning right. Here's why, as explained and dramatized by a candidate, now working at Microsoft, who fielded this puzzle in the early

1990s. The candidate actually stood up, pulled put his car key, and acted out the motions:

> I assume that most automobile buyers, like most people in the world, are right-handed, so let's design this car to meet the needs of the majority of consumers. I extend my right hand, holding a car key like this, with the key between my thumb and pointer finger. Now, I turn my hand clockwise as far as it can turn without discomfort. I can probably turn my wrist a full 180 degrees. Now let's try the motion counterclockwise. There is much less range of motion, maybe less than 90 degrees. I also seem to have less strength near the limit of the turn. The design of the hand, wrist, and arm thus makes it easier for a right-handed person to turn a key clockwise (that is, to the right). This analysis suggests that because it's easier for right-handed people to turn the key clockwise, turning the key to the right is the preferred design.

If you think about it for a moment, there's a Zen paradox here. Since the frequency of locking a car is the same as the frequency of unlocking a car, one of these motions is going to be "easy" and the other will be "awkward." On what basis should we decide to make the act of unlocking the car the easy motion? Is it as arbitrary as it appears? Perhaps not.

Extra credit: It makes sense to assign the easy motion to *unlocking* or opening the car door. There are life-and-death situations that call for being given every advantage to unlock the car. A mugger might be stalking you in the parking lot. An extra second may be the difference between being victimized and escaping. People with arthritis need every advantage to open locks. Even people with full strength in their wrists sometimes have trouble unlocking car doors when they freeze. For all these reasons, giving the majority of consumers every advantage to unlock their automobiles inclines designers to open car doors by turning to the right.

17 REFRIGERATOR IN A ROOM

A nice thought experiment that allows candidates to repurpose a common consumer item.

You are locked into an empty room with only a working refrigerator plugged into a standard electric outlet. The room is uncomfortably warm, and your goal is to cool the room to the maximum extent possible. What can you do?

Most candidates immediately think about opening the refrigerator to cool the room down. You can admit to that thought, but be wary. First of all, first impressions are never correct. Second, think deeper. What does a refrigerator really do? It's really a heat pump. It takes heat away from the contents of the refrigerator and empties the heat into the room. Opening the door of an operating refrigerator would be the worst move. Here's one candidate's response:

> Pull the plug on the refrigerator, and then open it. This will even out the lower temperature in the refrigerator with the higher temperature of the room, which will drop a little. The stupidest thing to do is to open the refrigerator without pulling its plug. It will then suck the heat of the room into its cooling compartment and get rid of it again through the cooling ribs on its backside, adding even more heat in the process. Being open, the cooling compartment will never be cold enough to trip the thermostat, and the fridge will be running constantly, in effect acting as an oven.

Solution: Unplug the refrigerator and open the door, allowing the cooler air in the refrigerator compartment to cool the room air a little bit. That's the best you can do.

18 WEIGHT ON MOON AND EARTH

Why should such a simple question create such complexities? Experience shows that if a candidate doesn't immediately get the solution to this puzzle, it is very unlikey he or she will ever get it without a hint. The trap here is that the mind immediately goes to the main difference between the earth and the moon—the difference in gravitational pull—and then stops there.

What weighs more on the moon than on the earth?

Hint: Think buoyancy.

Let's consider two excellent responses, one literal, one figurative.

First the literal. It takes a special mentality to move from one critical difference to consider what other differences may apply. In this case, the salient difference is that the moon has less gravity than the earth. True enough. But don't stop there. What other differences exist? Earth has an atmosphere and the moon does not. And what is one property of an atmosphere? It provides buoyancy. Things with definite mass definitely float on the earth and therefore have no weight. So, on the moon, any balloon filled with a lighter-than-air gas, such as helium or hydrogen, would work for an answer.

Some people may object that the balloon would nevertheless weigh as much on the moon as on earth. Granted the mass of the balloon remains unchanged, but weight is something else. On earth, helium balloons don't weigh anything because the atmosphere supports them. If you tried to put a helium-filled balloon on a scale, no weight would register because the buoyancy of the balloon is greater than the pull of gravity on the balloon. But on the moon, the moon's gravity would definitely pull it against a scale. Therefore, on the moon the balloon will actually register some weight, even with the moon's gravity one-sixth that of earth.

Extra credit: Note that it would be impossible to conduct this experiment. No inflatable balloon can exist on the moon or in a vacuum, as it will immediately explode.

Now a stunning metaphorical response voiced by my friend David Jones of Evanston, Illinois, proving that with the right attitude, every "technical" puzzle permits a satisfying nontechnical response:

> What weighs more on the moon than on the earth? The conscience of an astronaut, if the astronaut left for the moon on the morning of his wife's birthday and he forgot to acknowledge it.

Solution: Any lighter-than-air balloon or the conscience of an astronaut.

19 THE CORK AND BOTTLE

Some interviewers actually have a coin, bottle, and cork available as props as they pose this puzzle. If so, they act out the terms of the puzzle as they state it. But I recommend that puzzles stay in the abstract realm.

I'm going to put this coin in this bottle and then stop the opening of the bottle with this cork. Can you remove the coin without taking out the cork or breaking the bottle?

Hint 1: Waiters at restaurants solve this puzzle every day.

Hint 2: Let's say you're opening a wine bottle, and in the process you break the cork.

The out-of-the-box insight interviewers look for here is that the cork may be pushed *into* the bottle. Candidates who understand this are presumed to be able to address business problems in a jujitsu-like fashion, in which they use the strength of the problem against itself. Unfortunately, most candidates can't get past the bottleneck assumption that the cork must be extracted from the bottle.

Solution: Push the cork into the bottle and extract the coin.

20 GREAT PYRAMIDS OF EGYPT

This puzzle was used on the radio show Car Talk. *On one level, it is a trick question. But on another, it gives candidates who are not locked into assumptions a chance to shine. The puzzle can be quite perplexing to candidates who are locked into a particular mind-set.*

A young man took a trip to visit the Great Pyramids of Egypt in 1995. He was deeply moved by the trip and vowed that one day he would return with his children so that they could also see the wonders of the Great Pyramids. The man fulfilled his vow, and in 1969, he and his son visited the Great Pyramids. How is this possible?

Hint: How old are the Great Pyramids?

If you, as a candidate, find yourself speculating about time travel and being one's own grandfather, I have one word of advice: don't go there. These interview questions are *never* about fantasy. There is a solution here; you just have to get past the assumption, the mental blinders that are trapping you. The assumption is that the puzzle starts in AD 1995. Wrong. The puzzle actually is framed before the

32

Common Era, when the pyramids would still have been considered ancient.

Solution: The young man first visited the Great Pyramids in 1995 BC. In 1969 BC, 26 years later, he fulfilled his vow to his son.

21 HOW COLD IS IT?

This deceptively simple problem is so confusing in its statement that many candidates freeze up as they consider it. Its solution requires a bit of mental recalibration, a skill that is of inestimable value in business, where scaling problems often pop up.

What is the temperature when it's twice as cold as zero degrees?

Hint: Don't be confused by the word zero; *just reframe the puzzle by remembering that heat can be thought of as a liquid, that cold is a measure of the absence of heat, or that cold represents the slowing down of molecular motion.*

In order for this puzzle to make sense, the candidate must recalibrate the question. It's good to have some knowledge of the common temperature scales and how to convert among them. Often a conversation between the candidate and the interviewer is required. One candidate offered this exchange:

CANDIDATE: Before I answer that question, I need to understand the scale. Zero degrees in what scale?

The interviewer may specify a scale or say, "We're not sure."

CANDIDATE: Since "cold" is really just absence of heat, let's calculate how much heat we have to start with and then calculate half of that. We can calculate this problem in the familiar temperature scales of Fahrenheit and Celsius. The problem wouldn't make sense in the Kelvin scale, where 0 degrees Kelvin is also known as absolute zero at which point all heat is gone. So I'm assuming we are talking about a starting temperature above absolute zero. Nevertheless, it's convenient to work in the Kelvin scale. Absolute zero is about -273 degrees Celsius, or about -460 degrees Fahrenheit. So, starting in the Celsius scale, 0 degrees Celsius is 273 Kelvin. Half of that is 136.5 degrees Kelvin, or −136.5 degrees Celsius. In Fahrenheit, 0 degrees F is equivalent to 255.4 K. Twice as cold as 255.4 K is 127.7 K, or −230 degrees F.

Solution: 136.5 degrees K; −136.5 degrees C; −230 degrees F.

Extra credit: Mention that the absolute zero version of the Fahrenheit scale is the Rankine scale. Add 460 degrees to Fahrenheit temperatures to obtain the Rankine temperature. So 0 degrees Fahrenheit is 460 degrees Rankine, twice as cold of which becomes 230 degrees Rankine.

22 HOURGLASS WEIGHING

At first blush, this is reminiscent of the trick puzzle that goes, "What weighs more, a ton of bricks or a ton of feathers?" Of course, a ton is a ton. But is it? This pearl of a thought puzzle touches on some important elements of physics and logic.

An hourglass timer is being weighed on a sensitive scale, first when all the sand is in the lower chamber and then after the timer is turned over and the sand is falling. Will the scale show the same weight in both cases?

There are actually two plausible responses. One response is that falling grains are essentially weightless and exert no force on the scale as long as they are falling. Hence, the hourglass will weigh less after it is turned over. The other response is that from the instant that the first grain of falling sand strikes the bottom of the hourglass to the instant the last grain falls, the force resulting from the impact of the sand on the bottom of the glass remains constant and helps make the total weight equal to the weight of the hourglass before being inverted. When the stream begins to fall, the freely falling sand does not contribute to the weight, and so there is slightly less weight registered for the first few hundredths of a second. As the last grains of falling sand strike, there is a short time interval when the weight exceeds the initial weight. For each grain of sand now striking the bottom, no longer is there a grain of sand leaving the upper chamber, and so the hourglass weighs more.

Solution: In reality, the inverted hourglass weighs more.

23 TWO SURGICAL GLOVES, THREE PATIENTS

A perplexing problem framed in the antiseptic world of surgery. There is nothing theoretical about this solution. It can be implemented in the real world.

A one-armed surgeon needs to operate on three patients, one after another. But the surgeon has only two individual surgical gloves. How can the surgeon operate on the three patients in turn without risking infection for the patients or for himself?

Hint: Gloves are reversible.

Safety in this case necessitates that every operation requires a surgical glove whose surface has not been contaminated. This is for the protection of the patients as well as the surgeon. The interviewer is looking for you to find the "aha!" factor that will allow an elegant solution to this puzzle. Please don't even bother to think about creative ways to reuse surgical gloves.

To start, it's always good for the candidate to repeat the puzzle:

> Let me see if I have this. The situation is that the one-armed surgeon needs three clean gloves for three patients but has only two gloves. In other words, how can the surgeon operate safely with three patients using just two gloves? The gloves not only protect the patients from the surgeon, but ensure that no diseases are passed from one patient to the other.

I'm aware of only one satisfactory answer:

> The solution starts with the surgeon putting on two gloves, one over the other. She then operates on patient number 1. Then the surgeon removes the outermost glove, leaving the other one on. She now operates on patient number 2. Finally the surgeon takes the glove discarded from the surgery with patient number 1, reverses

it, and puts it on over the remaining glove. She can then operate on patient number 3.

The puzzle is actually more compelling in its original wording, involving a man with two condoms and three partners. It has been reworded here to work, more or less, in the present context. Don't even ask how a one-armed surgeon changes gloves.

Solution: Put on two gloves, one over the other, and then reverse the first glove.

24 THREE HIKERS

This is a puzzle that tests the use of resources. Most business problems involve similar estimations about priorities and resources.

Three friends are hiking to a remote destination in a wilderness area. The hike takes six days. Each person can carry only enough food and water for four days. Without sacrificing anyone or endangering anyone's life, the goal is to get as many people as possible safely to the destination. How many people can safely get to their destination?

The "aha!" factor is to understand that two of the hikers basically serve as food bearers to extend the range of the third hiker.

Call the hikers Tom, Dick, and Harry. Each hiker starts out with a four-day supply of food and water. After the first day, Tom gives a one-day supply to both Dick and Harry. This leaves Tom with a one-day supply to return to the starting point. Now Dick and Harry each have a four-day supply again. After the second day, Dick gives Harry a one-day supply and keeps a two-day supply for himself so that he can get safely back to the starting point. This gives Harry a four-day supply of food and water, sufficient for the four days remaining on his journey.

Solution: One hiker can make it.

25 GLASS HALF FULL

Ideally, the interviewer will use a water glass as a prop as this puzzle is presented. Sometimes a drawing of a water glass is offered.

Here's a glass of water. The water is in a transparent glass that is a perfect right cylinder. It appears that the glass is half full, but how can you really be sure? How can you accurately determine whether the glass is half full, more than half full, or less than half full? You have no rulers, writing utensils, or other tools.

Hint: Use the geometry of the cup.

Let's start off with a solution that most candidates think of first and examine why it's not good enough. Holding the glass upright, the candidate uses the palm of her left hand to cover the glass. Now she makes a pinching gesture with the index finger and thumb of her right hand. She puts her thumb at the base of the glass and her index finger adjacent to the water level, thereby gauging the height of the water surface from the base of the glass. Now she freezes the distance between her two fingers. She then flips the glass upside down with her left hand; no water falls out since she's sealed the opening with her left palm. Next she puts her frozen right hand, acting as a gauge, against the glass and checks to see if the inverted water level aligns with her index finger. If so, the glass is exactly half full. This may seem like a good solution, but it's actually inaccurate, because the palm of the hand is not a perfectly flat surface. Also, the technique will most likely lose some water in the inversion.

The most elegant solution requires the insight that the geometry of the glass offers an absolutely precise solution. The solution is easier to demonstrate than to describe. Carefully tilt the glass toward you so that the water almost spills out, but doesn't. The geometry of the glass (remember, it's a perfect right cylinder) is such that if the glass is exactly half full, the water level in the inside of the glass will be touching the upper inside rim of the bottom. If any of the inside bottom surface of the glass is exposed, the glass is less than half full. If the level is above the inside bottom ring of the glass, it is more than half full.

Solution: Exploit the inherent geometry of the glass by noting that a perfect right cylinder is half full at the point when the liquid level simultaneously touches the outside rim and inside rim of the glass.

26 HELP DESK! COW WON'T GIVE MILK

Koen van Tolhuyzen, a Web developer in Belgium, was confronted by this puzzle in a job interview in July 1999. "The interview started as a standard job interview," van Tolhuyzen recalls. "I had to give a small description of myself, my goals, my expectations. Then the interviewer said the following: 'I'm going to ask you a question that might sound very weird. I'll give you a few moments to think about it.' At first it looked kind of stupid. But afterwards I found it a very good question. You don't always have to ask technical questions to IT people to see if they are good candidates."

You're working in a help desk environment for farmers. At a certain moment, you get a phone call from a farmer who says, "My cow, who always stands in the middle of the grass, doesn't give any milk anymore." How will you try to detect and resolve the farmer's problem?

The goal of this interview question is to see if the candidate's problem-solving skills include the intuitive, creative, logical, analytical attributes that a good help desk technician requires. What happened is a role-playing scenario. The interviewer played the farmer, and the candidate got to ask questions. Van Tolhuyzen re-creates the exchange:

> At first I started asking questions about the cow, its age, color, etc. The interviewer always answered with "Let's say the cow is five years old, white, but that's totally irrelevant." Then I started asking questions about the current situation: "Have you had this problem before?" "Is the cow always in the middle of the grass?" "Where was she standing the last time when she did give milk?" When I established that the cow did give milk before, I looked for the changes in behavior or environment. That proved to be the key. The help desk is all about detecting changes in states.

In fact, there are no answers to this puzzle; there are only questions. But Leilani Allen of Mundelein, Illinois, a former chief information officer, rightly notes that the interviewer rigged the puzzle by declaring certain facts irrelevant. "Real help desk callers don't do that," she says. "The trick at help desks is to triage the questions to quickly identify what part of the system appears to be malfunctioning (e.g., hardware, software, user) and then ask the 'what changed' questions."

27 WHAT'S THE TEMPERATURE OUTSIDE?

This is an example of a projective puzzle. The clues are so scant that candidates basically have a blank canvas from which to work.

You are stuck inside an office building, and you want to know what the temperature is outside. How do you find out?

Hint: How far out is outside?

The way this puzzle is stated, with no specified constraints, tells the candidate that the interviewer is looking for as many potential solutions as possible. While the constraints are unstated, most candidates understand that it's not in their interests to have as their only response, "Break a window and put your hand (or a thermometer) outside," or "Watch the weather report on TV." In any case, the interviewer will shoot down the offered solutions. Nevertheless, start simple to test the unstated constraints of the problem. Whatever the candidate says, he or she should be prepared for an objection. Here's a typical scenario:

> CANDIDATE: Well you could use X to find the temperature.
>
> INTERVIEWER: OK, let's say there are no Xs lying around.
>
> CANDIDATE: OK, perhaps you could try Y.
>
> INTERVIEWER: Y is broken. What else?

Eventually, the candidate has to consider what "outside" means in this puzzle.

> CANDIDATE: I'm going to define "outside" as outside the atmosphere of the earth, in deep space, where the temperature is absolute zero.

Let's see the interviewer argue with that kind of vision! If the candidate is sufficiently outside the box, the solution becomes clear.

28 ROPE-CLIMBING MONKEY

Sometimes the interviewer will have a simple diagram of this puzzle.

A rope passes through a pulley. On one end of the rope is an iron weight. At the other end of the rope hangs a monkey of equal weight. What happens if the monkey starts to climb up the rope? (See Figure 3.3.)

Figure 3.3

Hint: Assume that this is a perfect machine—the pulley is frictionless, and the mass of the rope and pulley is negligible.

Start by considering the initial equilibrium situation, before the monkey starts to try to climb. The monkey's weight acts downward, pulling the rope with a force w, and the rope transfers this force directly to the weight on the other end of the rope, pulling the weight upward with a force w. However, the weight also pulls downward with an equal force w, which pulls the rope

40

with a force *w*, which acts on the monkey. Therefore both the weight and the monkey are pulled downward by their own weights and pulled upward by the rope with equal forces. This is why the situation is in equilibrium, and is why neither the monkey nor the weight move. Another way of saying all this is to say that the monkey balances the weight, so they don't move. Let a candidate who paid attention in physics class explain the rest:

> Now, what happens when the monkey tries to climb the rope? The monkey exerts an additional force on the rope, so it pulls the rope down with a force that is now greater than *w*. How is this possible? In exactly the same way as any person would climb any rope—when the person hangs from a rope, the rope is pulled by the person's weight, but when the person climbs it, he or she pulls the rope with a larger force. Hopefully, whatever is supporting the rope is strong enough not to break under this extra force and the person can climb the rope. This exertion of a greater force than one's weight happens every time someone does a chin-up, or in fact just stands up from the sofa.
>
> The monkey pulls the rope. On the other end of the rope, the weight is now pulled upward not just by the monkey's weight *w*, but by its climbing force too. It is only pulled downward by its own weight, *w*, though, so the net force is upward. Therefore the weight will accelerate upward.

Solution: The monkey is pulling down on the rope hard enough to pull itself up. This pulling action increases the effective weight of the monkey. The tension in the rope increases just enough to cause the weight to rise at the same rate as the monkey.

29 RECLAIMING ROPES

Sometimes the interviewer will have a simple diagram of this puzzle.

Two 50-foot ropes are suspended from a 40-foot ceiling, from hooks about 20 feet apart. If you are armed with only a knife, how much of the rope can you salvage?

Some candidates can solve this in their heads; others do well to draw it out first before answering. In fact, almost all the rope can be salvaged. Here's one response:

The answer is almost all of it. Here's how. Let's tie the ropes together. Now I climb up one of the ropes. As close as possible to the ceiling, I tie a loop in the rope. Now I cut the rope just below the loop. Now I run the rope through the loop and tie both ends to my waist. I can now swing to the other rope and climb that one. I now pull the rope going through the loop tight and cut the other rope as close as possible to the ceiling. I can now swing down on the rope through the loop. I lower myself to the ground by letting out rope. I retrieve the rope by untying it at my waist and pulling the rope through the loop. I now have all the rope except for the piece required for the loop.

Solution: Almost all of it.

30 WHICH IS THE MAGNET?

This is a puzzle that requires some knowledge of physics and magnetism.

You have two cylindrical rods of iron, identical in size and shape. One is a permanent magnet. The other is just nonmagnetized iron—attractable by magnets, but not a permanent magnet itself. Without any instruments, how can you determine which is which?

Take the two bars, and put them together like a T, so that one bisects the other (see Figure 3.4). If they stick together, then bar B is the magnet.

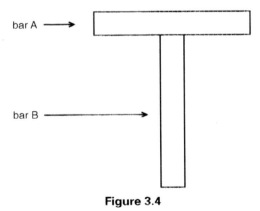

bar A

bar B

Figure 3.4

If they don't, bar A is the magnet. That's because bar magnets display no magnetic force at their centers since the two poles cancel out. So if bar A is the magnet, then bar B wouldn't be attracted to its center. However, bar magnets are quite alive at their edges (i.e., the magnetic force is concentrated). So if bar B is the magnet, then it will attract the iron of bar A at any point.

Solution: Configure the two magnets like a T.

31 CHAIN WITH 21 LINKS

This is a classic puzzle that appears in many puzzle books. But even candidates who've heard it before need to figure it out all over again each time they do it.

What is the least number of links you must cut in a chain of 21 links to be able to give someone all possible number of links up to 21?

Hint: Think factors.

Break down the problem, because the statement of the problem has two challenges: to calculate the least number of cuts and to calculate where those cuts are to be made. The key to the solution is to find the fewest numbers that can be combined to make 21. The answer is to cut links 4 and 10. What you end up with are three sections of 3, 5, and 11 links each, plus the 2 cut links that can serve as single-link units. To give all possible number of links up to 21:

    1: 1
    2: 1 + 1
    3: 3
    4: 3 + 1
    5: 5 or 3 + 1 + 1
    6: 5 + 1
    7: 5 + 1 + 1
    8: 5 + 3

9: 5+3+1

10: 5+3+1+1

11: 11

12: 11+1

13: 11+1+1

14: 11+3

15: 11+3+1

16: 11+5

17: 11+5+1

18: 11+5+1+1

19: 11+5+3

20: 11+5+3+1

21: 11+5+3+1+1

Solution: Two cuts at links 4 and 10.

32 GOLD CHAIN

Here's another chain puzzle requiring a slightly different mental leap.

You have a gold chain with seven links. You need to hire an assistant at a fee of one gold link per day for seven days. Each day, the assistant needs to be paid for his or her services without overpayment or underpayment. What is the fewest number of cuts to the chain to facilitate this arrangement?

Hint: Making change.

The major insight required for this puzzle is that the assistant is prepared to give change. It is not the case that you need to pay the assistant with one link at a time. The solution is to cut the third link. That cut will separate the chain to create three chains of four links, two links, plus the single cut link itself.

Day 1: Give the assistant the cut link.

Day 2: Take back the cut link; give the assistant the two-link chain.

Day 3: Give the assistant the cut link.

Day 4: Take back both the cut link and the two-link chain; give the assistant the four-link chain.

Day 5: Give the assistant the cut link.

Day 6: Take back the cut link, give the assistant the two-link chain.

Day 7: Give the assistant the cut link.

Solution: One cut, at the third link.

33 FREEZING SEVEN ICE CUBE TRAYS

Given the prevalence of icemakers in modern freezers, this puzzle sounds positively old-fashioned. Many young candidates have never seen an ice cube tray. But familiar or not, the puzzle calls for the ability to find an out-of-the-icebox solution.

You have an old-fashioned refrigerator with a small freezer compartment that could hold seven ice cube trays stacked vertically, but there are no shelves to separate the trays. You have an unlimited supply of trays, each of which can make a dozen cubes, but if you stand one tray on top of another before it's frozen, it will nest part way into the one below and you won't get full cubes from the bottom tray. Given these constraints, what is the fastest way to make ice cubes?

Hint: Building blocks.

Many situations require using the outcome of the process under consideration as a catalyst to solve the problem. The solution to this puzzle uses one of the outcomes. By using frozen cubes as spacers to hold the trays apart, you can make 84 cubes in the time it takes to freeze two trays. Here's how: Fill one tray, freeze it, and remove the cubes. Place two cubes in the opposite corners of six trays, and fill the rest with water. Freeze all six, plus a seventh you put on top, at the same time.

Solution: Use 12 frozen ice cubes as spacers to hold the trays apart.

34 ICE AND WATER

One interviewer likes to ask this question when the candidate is served a glass of water with ice in it.

Consider a glass of water with an ice cube in it and with the water level at the very brim of the glass. What happens to the water level as the ice melts? Will the water level go up and overflow the glass, go down, or remain unchanged. Why? Ignore evaporation and the effects of surface tension.

Most of us have encountered this situation before. As ice melts in a full glass, do we find that we need a napkin to mop up the overflow? The answer is no. But the important part of this puzzle is not the answer, but the explanation of why. Here's one candidate's response:

> Let me think out loud a minute. Ice is less dense than water. That's why it floats. We also know that ice occupies more volume than water. We know this because a full bottle of water will shatter as it freezes and the ice expands. So the first thought is that the water level will drop. But I know from experience that a glass full of ice doesn't overflow when the ice melts. Why is that? I think that's because the ice is floating with a section of the ice sticking up above the water level. Thus, when the ice melts, it shrinks, but this is counterbalanced by the volume of ice that is sticking up out of the water. Thus, there will be no change in the level of the water from the melting ice.

Solution: The water level is unchanged.

Extra credit: Note that if the ice were completely submerged, the water level would fall as the ice melted.

35 POLAR ICE CAPS MELTING

Here's another version of the Ice and Water puzzle, although with a strangely opposite answer. Again, the explanation is of more interest than the answer itself.

What will happen to the level of the oceans if the polar ice caps melt? Will the level of the oceans rise, fall, or remain the same?

The first thought is that if the polar ice caps melt, all the additional water will cause the oceans to rise. In this case, the first thought, so often a false start, is actually correct. If the world's ice melted, the water would flow into the ocean and raise the level significantly. In New York City, this would mean that the Atlantic Ocean would rise to the level of the sixteenth story of the Empire State Building.

So what's the difference between the polar ice caps melting and ice melting in a glass? In the latter case, the ice is floating. In the former, much of the polar ice caps, especially in Antarctica, is actually on land and thus not displacing ocean water.

Solution: The oceans would rise.

SCENARIOS

These puzzlelike scenarios were developed by Peter Herzog, managing director of the Institute for Security and Open Methodologies, to screen and train applicants for positions in network security. People responsible for security need to be able to think outside the box because the threats they are hired to thwart always come from people who operate outside the box. These scenarios have proved very effective in identifying applicants who have the creativity, analytical expertise, and observation skills that make for excellent security administrators, according to Herzog. The four steps in each scenario are carefully constructed to force candidates to think creatively. These are Herzog's general instructions:

> *In these scenarios, you are asked to assume different professions from electrician to postal worker to doctor and then answer the questions accordingly. Within each of these professions, I will ask*

you to describe methods for performing a task. Each scenario has four questions. Your answers should be brief and to the point.

After each set of answers, Herzog and the candidate talk about the answers. That's the whole point: the conversation that these scenarios prompt. The scenarios emphasize speed. Herzog gives candidates about a minute for each step. Contact information for Herzog and the Institute for Security and Open Methodologies can be found in Appendix E, "Additional Sources and Links."

36 SCENARIO 1—ELECTRICIAN

You are an electrician. In front of you is a light hanging from the ceiling, and behind you is a light switch on the wall. The light is currently on.

1. *List 10 ways to turn off the light.*
2. *List 10 components of a functioning light.*
3. *List 10 ways to tell if the light is off.*
4. *List 10 ways to prevent someone from being able to turn off the light.*

Herzog looks for candidates who have the fluidity of mind and confidence under stress to quickly rattle off plausible answers. Answers are rarely right or wrong, although some answers are clearly better than others. Herzog expects obvious answers as well as more creative ones. What he looks for most is a display that the candidate has a deep understanding of the processes involved. "They need to show me that they know there's a big picture behind a lightbulb," he says. For example, here are the five most common responses to the first question (10 ways to turn off the light):

1. Turn switch off.
2. Break bulb.
3. Rip out wiring.
4. Overload electricity.
5. Cut electricity to room.

The opportunities for conversation are rich. Some candidates come up with answers that are profound. For example, here's a response from a candidate with an understanding of social engineering:

Pay someone to turn off the light.

Is this candidate being cute or actually revealing an epistemological paradox about light:

Close your eyes.

Other responses reveal the special expertise of candidates. One with a background in quantum physics offered:

Devise an instrument to cancel the light by emitting light of the exact wavelength but opposite phase of the light from the lightbulb.

37 SCENARIO 2—POSTAL CARRIER

You are a postal carrier for an independent express postal service. You have a book-sized package to deliver.

1. *List 10 ways to identify the* receiver *of the package.*
2. *List 10 things that would stop you from delivering the package.*
3. *List 10 reasons for delivering the package at all.*
4. *List 10 ways to identify the* sender *of the package.*

38 SCENARIO 3—RECORD STORE OWNER

You own an independent record store, which grew out of your intense fascination with music. The success of your store depends on your customers, who are also music enthusiasts.

1. *List 10 ways to categorize the records in the store.*
2. *List 10 ways to identify the musical tastes of a customer.*
3. *List 10 ways to protect your inventory from theft.*
4. *List 10 things that would influence a customer not to buy from you.*

39 SCENARIO 4—SOLDIER

You are a solider in full field gear during wartime. You are stationed at the only bridge that crosses over a gorge.

1. *List 10 ways to prepare for the coming enemy.*
2. *List 10 ways to prevent the enemy from crossing the bridge.*
3. *List 10 ways to discern friendly bridge users from the enemy.*
4. *List 10 problems the enemy could cause if they crossed the bridge.*

Herzog recalls one pertinent response to question 1: Build a million bridges over the gorge and line all but one of the bridges with explosive mines. Only the allies know which bridge is safe to cross. This answer corresponds to an actual network security strategy for wireless networks, which protects one true node by constructing millions of virtual nodes that lead to nothing.

40 SCENARIO 5—SAFETY INSPECTOR

You are a licensed safety inspector for an independent occupational safety consortium. You have been brought to a large factory to review the safety of the machine tools due to a high number of accidents.

1. *List 10 questions you would ask the foreman of this factory.*
2. *List 10 concerns the employees may have with the current rise in accidents.*
3. *List 10 changes that would make the factory a safer place to work.*
4. *List 10 concerns the employees may have with the implemented changes.*

41 SCENARIO 6—COMPUTER HELP DESK SUPPORT PERSON

You work telephone help desk support for a large corporation dedicated to assisting its employees with support questions worldwide. You are the front line of defense, which means you receive all support matters.

1. List 10 questions you may ask to diagnose the problem.

2. List 10 resources you could use to solve the problem.

3. List 10 concerns the caller may have with following your advice.

4. List 10 ways you can assure better service.

42 TAPERED COKE CANS

This Microsoft favorite has shown up on countless job interviews and has become totally overused. Yet like bell bottoms from the 1960s, these puzzles once thought hopelessly out of fashion will make a comeback. Gerry Bollman, director of university recruiting, Booz-Allen & Hamilton, Cleveland, agrees that the Coke can question makes sense for a manufacturing or operational process position. For technical positions, the puzzle is designed for the candidate to display some creativity and engineering savvy in a new knowledge domain. Even though I am not satisfied that this puzzle is useful for jobs other than perhaps beverage container manufacturing, it is included here because it was at one time so popular and can reappear.

Why are Coke and beer cans tapered at the top and bottom?

Hint: What issue are process-oriented operations most concerned with?

To this question, the inevitable responses of almost all candidates go to increasing the strength of cans, especially to resist internal pressure of the carbonated contents. This response is not inaccurate, but like all obvious answers, it is not the complete picture. The first generations of Coke and beer cans were not originally tapered; nor were the tapers added to make the cans stronger. The bottoms and tops of cans are now tapered less for engineering reasons than for business reasons. The tapers allow the cans to be made with just a little less material and so save costs. Across billions of cans, these micro savings add up to big bucks.

Now that the cans used the thinnest possible amount of aluminum, engineers had a problem with the top. Architecturally, the strongest part of the can needs to be the top to withstand the strong stresses of the consumer forcing open the flip top. For this reason, manufacturers found it necessary to minimize the top's diameter. This step required adding a bevel to connect the top of the can to the slightly larger diameter of the can itself. This bevel represents the taper at the top. As for the bottom, cans need to be symmetrical so they can stack easily.

The Microsoft blogs are full of anecdotes about the Coke (sometimes Pepsi) can questions. First, the response of a software engineer who got the job:

> I'm pretty sure the reason is strength. The difference between pop and vegetables (which are canned in straight-sided cans) is the pressure inside. Hopefully it won't be too great at the moment you pop the top, but shake the cans up inside a hot semitrailer truck for a few hours and the pressure gets pretty high. That's also why they have concave bottoms, and how it happens that you sometimes get a can with the bottom bulging out; think of the pressure it takes to do that.

Now here's a college junior who applied for an internship at Microsoft. He didn't get it. Can you guess why?

> I assume sharp, square corners could not handle the pressure as well. The rounder a body, the better it withstands inside (or outside) pressure. A sphere, however, isn't practical. To stack the cans, and place them on a table without having them role off, they need to be relatively flat at top and bottom. So tapering the ends of the cylinderlike can gives the best overall result.

REASONING PUZZLES THAT DON'T REQUIRE MATH

For many interviewers, the best puzzles for job interviews rely on logic alone. Puzzles that require calculations are not as useful because they often don't generate the quality of conversations that interviewers want. Either the candidate knows the math or he or she doesn't. And while interviewers welcome sharp math skills, they value other qualities—intuition, creativity, vision—even more. All these puzzles can be solved in less than three minutes by most candidates. In most cases, a mathematical solution also exists, and if it is simple enough, the equations are also presented. But in all cases, the intuitive approach is preferred to a rigorous solution.

43 THREE COLOR JELLY BEANS

This is a simple, nonthreatening puzzle that is good for a warm-up. It is often used by recruiters conducting telephone interviews.

You have a bucket of jelly beans in three colors: red, green, and blue. With your eyes closed, you have to reach in the bucket and take out two jelly beans of the same color. How many individual jelly beans do you have to take to be certain of getting two of the same color?

Hint: No color specified.

Most people will get this pretty quickly without the need for a hint or asking questions. The answer is four. The worst case is that the first three selections will yield jelly beans of unique colors. But since there are only three colors, the fourth pick must necessarily yield duplication.

Solution: Four jelly beans.

Extra credit: Note the general rule, that with n colors, you will always have two of one color if you grab $(n+1)$ jelly beans.

44 BLACK SOCKS, WHITE SOCKS

This problem is similar to the jelly bean puzzle, but there's an added element of uncertainty and a hidden clue.

There are three sock drawers in a bureau. The drawers are labeled White, Black, and Mixed, but every drawer is labeled incorrectly. One drawer has all white socks, one all black socks, and one mixed white and black socks. You are permitted to close your eyes and pick one sock from one drawer. How can you correctly label each drawer?

Hint: What does the label say?

Absolutely essential is to realize the significance of the clue that every drawer is labeled *incorrectly*. Once that's understood, the optimum strategy is to pick a sock from the drawer (incorrectly) labeled Mixed. Inspect the sock. If it is a white sock, then the drawer must be full of white socks. Why? Because it can't be the Mixed drawer (for then it would be correctly labeled in the first place). The labels on the two remaining drawers are simply exchanged. If it is a black sock, then the drawer gets the Black label. The labels on the two remaining drawers are simply exchanged. The powerful clue that every drawer is incorrectly labeled allows the problem to be solved with just one inspection.

Solution: Select from the Mixed sock drawer.

Interviewer Ole Eichorn is tough on programming candidates who can't figure this puzzle out: "What I like about this puzzle is that it is a simple matter of working through a fixed number of choices, and this challenge comes up in programming design all the time. As with the Contaminated Pills puzzle [see puzzle 69], I really would expect to be able to coax a candidate through this problem successfully. Actually the puzzle is pretty easy, so I would hope they could figure it out for themselves."

Microsoft interviewers have been known to frame this puzzle in the following way:

> There are three vending machines dispensing, according to the signs, Coke, Sprite, and Coke or Sprite. Each of the machines is labeled incorrectly. One can costs a quarter. How many quarters do you need to correctly label the three vending machines?

Obviously, one quarter in the Coke or Sprite vending machine will do the trick.

45 WHAT COLOR IS THE LAST MARBLE?

A classic marble selection puzzle.

In a box you have 13 white marbles and 15 black marbles. You also have 28 black marbles outside the box. Remove 2 marbles, randomly, from the box. If the marbles are of different colors, put the white one back in the box. If they are of the same color, remove both of them and replace them with a black marble from outside the box. Continue this process until only 1 marble remains in the box. What color is the last marble?

Hint: Selecting in pairs.

Some interviewers prefer candidates who solve this problem intuitively as opposed to the brute force method other candidates use. One interviewer thought this candidate's response was ideal:

> Since marbles can only be taken out in pairs and we started off with an odd number of white marbles, there is always going to be 1 white marble left over that you'll keep putting back in the box until it's left on its own.

Solution: The last marble will be white.

46 LILY PAD

These two puzzles speak to an understanding of geometric progression.

A lily pad doubles in size every day. If on the sixtieth day the pond is totally covered with lily pads, on what day is the pond half covered?

Hint: Plot the changes day by day.

For many applicants, the first thought is 30 days. Repeat the wording of the puzzle to yourself and work backward. If the pond is covered on the sixtieth day, what is the condition of the pond on the previous day? If the lily pad doubles in size every day, it is on the day before the last day that the pond is half covered.

Solution: The fifty-ninth day.

The puzzle can be reworded in the following way. Somehow scaling the problem in years instead of days makes it even harder.

A tree doubles in height each year until it reaches its maximum height in 20 years. How many years does it take this tree to reach half its maximum height?

Solution: 19 years.

47 BUS STOP PUZZLE

Many people already know this excellent puzzle that looks at a candidate's moral/ethical thinking. But for those who don't, the puzzle represents a real challenge as well as the opportunity to explore issues of altruism, loyalty, and self-interest. Some people regard this as an example of a lateral thinking puzzle. But to me, the puzzle has nothing missing. There's no right or wrong here, but one solution is so inescapably elegant that anything else pales in comparison.

A young man is driving along in his two-seater sports car on a stormy night. He passes a bus stop and sees three people waiting for the bus:

- *An elderly woman who is in serious distress and needs to get to the hospital or she will die.*
- *A best friend from the Army who once saved his life.*
- *An attractive person who may be the young man's soul-mate.*

The young man's car accommodates only two people. What do you think he should do in this situation?

Hint: Question your assumptions. Why does the driver have to stay with the car?

This puzzle requires candidates to accept that the issue is about ethics. Avoid speculating about when the bus will come or cramming everyone into the car. The issue is about balancing competing interests and making a choice and living with the consequences, a situation that is common to all businesses. So let's look at the ethical claims here. The first impulse for many candidates is to consider the plight of the elderly woman who will die. This is desirable. These candidates will pick up the woman and take her to the hospital. Candidates who respond to loyalty will want to pick up the old friend as payback for saving the young man's life. Few candidates will selfishly drive off with the potential soulmate, leaving the elderly woman to die and the best friend as a witness. But in the unlikely event the candidate does pick the soulmate, the interviewer will object by saying, "What, and take the chance that you'll never find your perfect life partner again?"

The goal is to find an out-of-the-box solution that balances all the interests. But, quick, what assumptions are you making? Not challenging the unstated assumption—in this case that you must stay with the sports car—is what makes this puzzle so interesting. As soon as that assumption is deflated, the solution comes more easily.

Solution: The young man stops the car, gives the car keys to his best friend, and asks him to drive the elderly lady to the hospital for immediate treatment. The young man stays behind and waits for the bus with the attractive person of his dreams.

48 $21 BETWEEN THEM

This problem is often found in puzzle books for children. But it can trip up adults, who tend to think the problem is harder than it is. It can serve as a warm-up for something more rigorous. While there's a little trivial arithmetic behind this puzzle, the leap required for its solution is not mathematical.

Betty has $20 more than Sally. How much does each have given that, combined, they have $21 between them? Note: You can't use fractions in the answer.

Hint: Convert dollars to cents.

Why does this problem give smart people such vapor lock? Maybe it's reminiscent of the impossible trick questions we all received in grade school. Maybe it's the constraint about "no fractions."

So people struggle. The obvious solution is that Betty has $21 and Sally has $1. Like all obvious solutions, this one is incorrect. It satisfies the first condition, but not the second. Their funds add up to $22. Some candidates actually consider the correct solution—Betty has $20.50 and Sally has $0.50—and then get confused with the "no fractions" rule. But why? Who says cents are fractions?

The point of the puzzle is to give the only reasonable solution and have confidence in your response. The actual solution is that Betty has $20.50 and Sally has $0.50. For those so inclined to use a little algebra, here are the equations. Dollars are converted into cents. Let S = Sally and B = Betty:

$$B = S + 2000¢$$
$$B + S = 2100¢$$

Hence,

$$B = 2050¢$$
$$S = 50¢$$

But to my mind, a candidate who whips out simultaneous equations to solve this problem reveals a certain rigidity in thinking. Interviewers much prefer candidates who can noodle this puzzle out without going through all that rigmarole.

Solution: Betty has $20.50, and Sally has $0.50.

49 PADLOCKS AND CRYPTOGRAPHY

Puzzles involving locks and boxes are well known, but still require a bit of thought. This is one of the simplest variations. These puzzles have the added advantage of referencing public key encryption strategies, a demonstrated knowledge of which may make a candidate more desirable.

You want to send a valuable object to a friend securely. You have a box that is more than large enough to contain the object. You have several locks with keys. The box has a locking ring that is more than large enough to have a lock attached. But your friend does not have the key to any lock that you have. How do you send the object securely?

Hint: Note the implied constraint: you cannot send a key in an unlocked box since the key might be copied en route.

This puzzle has a direct application in cryptography. Let's say you want to send a secret message to your friend. Because you don't trust commercial and freeware encryption methods, you use a secret cipher of your own. Only you know the key to the cipher. Not even your friend knows it. So you send the encrypted message; your friend encrypts it further with his or her favorite secret cipher and sends it back to you. You remove your cipher and send it back to your friend; and he or she removes the second secret cipher and reads the clear text. This process has the benefit of being very quick and easy by e-mail.

The above story of the locked box is often told as an introduction to public key cryptography. The ideas are perhaps related in some ways. But the story may just be told to show that really secure ciphers (ones where the decryption keys are not spread around to many people) are possible.

Solution: Put the valuable object into the box, secure it with one of your locks, and send the box to your friend. Your friend should then attach one of his own locks and return it. When you receive it again, remove your lock and send it back. Now your friend can unlock his own lock and retrieve the object.

50 ODDLY DIVIDED COINS

This is an old recreational bar puzzle, but it lends itself well to job interviews. Some interviewers actually have props for candidates to manipulate.

Can you put the 10 pennies shown in Figure 4.1 into the three glasses in such a way that each glass contains an odd number of pennies?

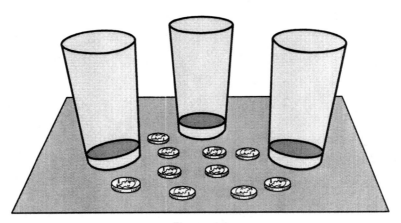

Figure 4.1

The first thing candidates need to understand is that, as stated, the problem is incapable of solution. Dividing 10 pennies among three glasses so each glass holds an odd number of pennies is impossible because any three odd numbers added together yields an odd number. The trick here is to change the arrangement of the glasses so a penny could count as being in more than one glass at a time. By placing an even number of pennies into a glass, an odd number of pennies into a second glass, and then placing the second glass into the first, both glasses contain an odd number of pennies (see Figure 4.2).

Figure 4.2

Solution: A number of solutions are possible. One solution calls for 2 pennies in one glass, 3 pennies inside a glass within the first glass, and 5 pennies in the third glass.

51 RED-PAINTED CUBE

This puzzle will be easy for candidates who have talent for spatial orientation. Others will need to go through a brute force solution. The puzzle may be worded as a probability problem, but it is included in this chapter instead of Chapter 6 because elementary logic trumps everything else.

A 3-inch cube is painted on all sides with red paint. The cube is then cut into small cubes of dimension 1 inch. All the cubes so cut are collected and thrown on a flat surface. What is the probability that all the top-facing surfaces have red paint on them?

The key to solving this problem is to visualize a cube cut into three sections. The core of the 3-inch cube when cut is a cube with all internal faces and as such has none of its faces painted red. Hence, one cube with no painted face always occurs, making the probability of having all red faces zero.

Solution: The probability is zero.

52 HANDS ON A CLOCK

Amazingly, this puzzle works well even if there is a wall-mounted analog clock in the room. Puzzles about the most familiar objects in our lives frequently trip us up (see also the next puzzle).

Consider an analog clock. What is the angle between the minute hand and the hour hand at 3:15?

Hint: No, it's not 0.

> Okay, there are 12 hours on the clock making 360 degrees, so each hour represents 30 degrees. At 3 p.m., the hour hand is directly on the 3 and the minute hand is directly on the 12. After 15 minutes, or one-quarter of an hour, the hour hand will have moved one-quarter of the 30 degree arc, or 7.5 degrees from the minute hand. The minute hand will now be on the 3. So the hour hand will be 7.5 degrees away from the minute hand.
>
> *Solution:* 7.5 degrees.

Extra credit: How many times per day do the hour and minute hands of an analog clock form a right angle?

First, let's consider the obvious answer. The hands of a clock form a right angle twice an hour (at a quarter to and a quarter past the hour). So with 24 hours in a day, that means the hands will form a right angle 48 times a day. Right? Not quite. Between 2:00 and 3:00 and then between 3:00 and 4:00, only one right angle is formed. Check it out yourself. So that means subtracting 4 (for both a.m. and p.m.) from the total.

Solution: 44 times.

53 OVERLAPPING CLOCK HANDS

Here's another clock-face geometry problem. Few people will get the right answer to this puzzle. No matter. Thinking creatively about the puzzle and getting close is good enough for most interviewers.

Consider an analog clock. How many times a day do a clock's hands overlap?

Nothing could be simpler, right? Watch out! The obvious thought is that clock hands overlap 12 times a day. Then if you're clever, you realize you have to double that conclusion, or 24 times a day. But that's way too easy, so there must be a catch. If you think about it intuitively you'll eventually conclude that the minute hand overtakes the hour hand somewhat less than once per hour. The obvious solution would be true only if the hour hand remained stationary, but, of course, the hour hand progresses at about ½ the rate of the minute hand. So a back-of-the-envelope solution suggests that the clock hands overlap every 1½ hours or every 65 minutes.

While not exactly right, this solution is close. If the candidate gets this far, most interviewers will want to move on. But if the interviewer asks the candidate to be sure or prove it, the explanation will go something like this, according to Roger Breisch of Batavia, Illinois:

> Let's think about the number of degrees traveled by each hand of the clock. As we know, a circle has 360 degrees. The minute hand travels 360 degrees per hour. The hour hand travel 360 degrees in 12 hours or 30 degrees per hour. Then the question is how long for the minute hand to "catch" the hour hand if the hour hand has a 360 degree head start?
>
> Let x be the number of hours it takes the minute hand to catch the hour hand plus go an additional 360 degrees. So the degrees traveled by the minute hand (x hours · 360 degrees/hour) must equal the degrees traveled by the hour hand PLUS 360 (x hours · 30 degrees/hour + 360 degrees).

x hours · 360 degrees/hour =

x hours · 30 degrees/hour + 360 degrees

$360x = 30x + 360$

$330x = 360$

$x = 1.090909$ or $1\frac{1}{11}$ hours

Then 24 divided by 1.090909 or $1\frac{1}{11}$ = 22 overlaps per day.

A much simpler solution comes from the nimble mind of Katherine Lato of Warrenville, Illinois. A trainer at Lucent Technologies, Lato manages to make the clock-hands problem look trivial. Her solution is ingenious if not exactly rigorous, and I'm not sure it really proves anything, but I'd hire her in a New York minute. Let's show her logic:

> The solution is calculated by recognizing that the minute hand will go around an analog clock face 24 times in 24 hours, and the hour hand will go around 2 times in 24 hours. Since both hands travel in the same direction—clockwise—the minute hand will overtake the hour hand 24 − 2 times or 22 overtakes per day.

Solution: Every 1¹⁄₁₁ hours, or 22 times a day.

54 FOR WHOM THE BELL TOLLS

Another clock puzzle, but of a decidedly different flavor. The simpler the puzzle, the more sure you are of the answer, the more you need to think it through. There's no better example of this truism than this puzzle.

The bells of the clock tower take 5 seconds to signal six o'clock with 6 loud rings. How long will it take for the bells to signal twelve o'clock noon?

Hint: It's not 10 seconds. If it were, this wouldn't be much of a puzzle, would it?

The puzzle requires an understanding that the time represents not the rings but the periods between the rings. The 5 seconds needed to signal six o'clock represent the 5 silent intermissions between rings. At noon, the 12 rings are separated by 11 silent intermissions, which need 11 seconds to be executed.

Solution: 11 seconds.

55 GENERAL RULE FOR FAIR DIVISION OF A PIE

Every child knows that there's a fair way for two people who do not trust each other to divide a pie. The technique requires the first person to cut the pie while the second person chooses which piece to take. Self-interest will ensure that the person doing the cutting divides the pie fairly.

The challenge is to generalize this division technique to more than two people. How can, say, five people, or n people, who do not necessarily trust each other, divide a pie so that everyone receives an equal share?

Hint: Think slivers, not pieces, of pie.

Number the people from 1 to *n*. Person 1 cuts off a piece of the pie. This piece of pie now becomes the subject of a process such that one of the people will eventually have to accept it as his or her share of the pie. In this process, person 2 can either pass or slice off an additional piece of pie. Then person 3 has the same two choices, followed by person 4, etc., until the last person has had a turn. The person who last touched the piece of pie must accept it as his or her share and is then removed from the process. Then another person cuts a piece of the pie, and the process is repeated until everyone has a piece.

If the first person cuts off an unfairly large piece of pie, other people will diminish it until it seems fair but not smaller than fair because they would then be at risk of being the last one to touch it. Thus greed is checked by a generalized process that rewards people acting fairly.

Extra credit: Discuss how to ensure that no one can be cheated by a coalition of the others.

56 CUTTING THE CAKE

There are two answers to this geometric puzzle, and if you're good, you would do well to identify both of them. But do them in the order presented here—the first one first and then the other.

How do you cut a rectangular cake into two equal pieces when someone has already removed a rectangular piece of any size or orientation from it? You are allowed just one straight cut.

Hint: The center will hold.

For most people, either they know how to conceptualize the geometry of this puzzle or they don't. The insight is to understand how to bisect nesting rectangles (see Figure 4.3). Ole Eichorn, on his blog *The Critical Connection* (http://w-uh.com/), offers this analysis:

> This question definitely has a right answer. The key insight is knowing or realizing that any line passing through the center point of a rectangle bisects the rectangle. Before you remove the rectangular piece from the cake, there are infinitely many lines that bisect the cake. After you remove the rectangular piece, there is only one—the line that passes through both the center of the cake and the center of the removed rectangular piece. This line necessarily divides the removed piece in half, and hence the same amount of cake was removed from each half of the remaining portion.
>
> The value in this question is not only seeing if candidates can compute the answer, but watching them eliminate nonsolutions. The fact that there is no constraint on the location of the removed rectangular piece is key. Perhaps they will ask for constraints ("Can I assume the removed piece is along an edge?"). I wouldn't say "no." Rather, I'd say "In what way is that helpful?" They would probably realize after a little trial-and-error that such a constraint is not helpful, and that might guide them toward the solution.

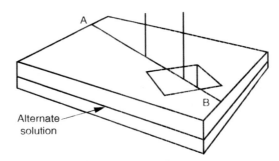

Figure 4.3 *The line AB connects the centers of the exterior and interior rectangles.*

Now for the alternate solution. Most people will think only of vertical cuts. Some bright thinkers believe they are operating "outside the box" when they propose the solution of simply slicing the cake horizontally to create two equal layers (alternate solution). But every grade school child would criticize this solution because everyone who prefers icing knows that the tops and bottoms of cakes are not and never will be equal. More critically, if the interior rectangular cut is oriented on an angle, the solution is incorrect. Nevertheless, most interviewers give candidates credit for suggesting the horizontal cut. "I'd say this solution gets points for creativity, but I'd still want to see the candidate solve the problem the other way," Eichorn says.

57 DRAGON VERSUS KNIGHT

This was used as an interview puzzle by Austin, Texas–based Trilogy Software. It seems a bit complicated for a job interview puzzle, but it does offer opportunities for a good conversation about strategy. A candidate who can make sense of this puzzle should do well juggling the terms of complicated business deals. It is reminiscent of a celebrated duel-by-drinking-poison scene in the 1987 movie The Princess Bride.

A dragon and a knight are trapped on a desert island. This island has seven poisoned wells, numbered 1 to 7. If they drink from a well, they can save themselves only by drinking from a higher number well within a few minutes' time. Well 7 is located at the top of a high mountain, so only the dragon can reach it. In other words, if the dragon drinks from well 4, it will die unless it has a cup of poison from wells 5 to 7. The same is true of the knight. One day they decide that the island isn't big enough for the two of them, and they have a duel. Both the knight and dragon are rational creatures. Each of them brings a cup of water to the duel, they exchange cups, and both drink the contents of the cup brought by his adversary. After the duel, the knight lives and the dragon dies. What strategy did the knight use to defeat the dragon?

Hint: Think not only outside the box but outside the island.

Let's review the facts. Both the dragon and the knight know that the knight cannot reach well 7. The dragon therefore probably fills its cup from well 7 knowing that the knight could not get an antidote to the water from that well. The knight figures this out and so prepares himself with a cup of water from well 1. First he drinks water from well 1 (weakest poison), and then he quickly drinks water from the dragon's glass, which probably contains water from a higher number well. Then he quickly drinks from the well 1 cup again, and then he quickly drinks water from well 2. That way, if the dragon offered him water from wells 2 to 7 the knight simply poisoned and cured himself twice. If the dragon gave him water from well 1, then what actually happened was that he drank water from well 1 and then water from well 2—which would save him. For his strategy, the knight gives the dragon a cup filled from water surrounding the island. The dragon, thinking it got a cup of poison from well 1 (or up to well 6), drank it and then immediately drank from well 7, as an antidote to a presumed poisoning. But since the dragon, in fact, drank seawater and not poisoned water, drinking from well 7 poisoned it fatally.

Solution: Give the dragon sea water.

58 PARACHUTIST IN THE DARK

This is a relatively new brainteaser that candidates in the Midwest have been given. No doubt there are solutions other than the two mentioned here. If you can think of a better answer, please let me know.

You are a parachutist landing in total darkness on an island of unknown shape. You know there is a fenced lot somewhere on the island. Your challenge is to determine whether you have landed within the fenced lot or outside the fenced lot.

Hint: You have a parachute, with lots of string.

The simplest solution is for the parachutist to walk in a straight line and count the number of fences he has to climb until he hits water. If the number of times he climbed a fence is odd, he landed inside the fence; if it's even, he landed outside. But the interviewer may have a few objections to this solution. The island may be very large, and the parachutist may wander around forever. Also, the solution does not consider the parachute as a tool.

Interviewers like candidates to honor the principle of conservation of clues. In other words, if the puzzle includes a clue (like a parachute), the candidate should really make use of it in the solution. In this vein, another solution is to tie all the parachute string together to make a long rope. Then the parachutist walks until he finds a fence. He doesn't know if it's an inside fence or outside fence. He then follows the fence, stringing the rope behind him. When he comes to the starting point and encounters the string, he pulls the two ends. If the rope tightens up, he is outside the fence; if the rope collapses, he is inside the fence.

The interviewer may object: Your string solution assumes the fenced area is purely convex. If it has concave sections, then the string would collapse even if you were outside. You could solve both of these objections by stipulating that the fence has continuous positive curvature. Then it would be possible to tie the long-as-possible string to the fence, follow the fence until you run out of string, and feel how the string is oriented with respect to the fence. If the string is plastered against the fence, then you're on the outside; otherwise if it separates from the fence, you're on the inside.

59 BOEING 747

This is another oldie-but-goodie brainteaser that generations of Microsoft candidates have had to face. Chances are you won't get this problem at Microsoft anymore, but it's still instructive. It could have been listed as one of the gross order of estimation problems in Chapter 9, but since this one has a "right" answer and a couple of elegant solutions that will actually get you surprisingly close, it's listed here.

How would you weigh a Boeing 747 without using scales?

Hint: Displacement or tire pressure.

There are many solutions to this puzzle. For many interviewers, the intended response is that you put the jet on a large boat, say an aircraft carrier, and paint a mark on the hull where the water line is. Now remove the jet and the boat rises in the water. Finally, load the boat with items of known weight, say one hundred 100-pound bags of cement, until the boat sinks to the waterline mark you previously painted. The total weight of the items loaded on the boat equals the weight of the jet.

Dale Fedderson, a career counselor at a Los Angeles–based career center, considers the following solution even more elegant. As a former teacher, he used this technique to get his students to measure the weight of his automobile. Fedderson explains:

> Measure the square inches of tire rubber contacting the tarmac for all tires (easy to do with a ruler and a thin straightedge), measure the tire pressure, and multiply pressure times square inches. That is the total weight of the plane. In the case of a Boeing 747-400, assume there are 16 landing gear tires and two nose gear tires, with each tire representing 175 square inches of tarmac contact. Further, assume the tire pressure to be 125 pounds per square inch. The calculation, then, is 18 tires · 175 square inches · 125 pounds per square inch = 393,750 pounds.
>
> Because a tire is a flexible support, so long as the vehicle is not actually resting on the rims, the rubber contacting the road is all that holds it up, and the rubber does that by pressure—"pounds per square inch"—which necessarily has to counteract and be equal to the weight of the vehicle.

Smart-aleck responses, such as looking up the technical specifications for the 747 on the Boeing Web site, are not recommended. In fact, the specifications are there, and they reveal that the typical operating (empty) weight for a Boeing 747-400 is 398,780 pounds (an answer that corresponds amazingly well with Fedderson's calculation).

Solution: Many solutions are possible. Two agreeable ones are to calculate weight by displacement of water or combined air pressure on tires.

Extra credit: The weight of the plane can also be derived this way: Calculate the volume of that portion of the ship between the first water level (without the jet) and the second water level (with the jet). Multiply that volume by the density of water, and you will also get the weight of the jet.

60 THREE LIGHT SWITCHES

A classic logic puzzle, but one so elegant that it deserves a place in the pantheon of logic puzzles.

There are three switches in a hallway. One switch controls a light fixture in a room at the far end of the hall. The door to the room is closed, and you can't see whether the light is on or off. You need to find out which of the three switches controls the light. You are allowed only one inspection. How can you be certain of finding out which switch controls the light?

Hint: Lightbulbs also do this.

The chief constraint is that you are allowed only one inspection. In other words, you need to solve the brainteaser with one and only one opportunity to obtain clues. Many candidates spoil their chances by wasting credibility on trying to defeat the constraint, e.g., Can I set up a video camera? Can I keep the door open? It's much better to accept the constraint and work within it.

Call the switches 1, 2, and 3. Leave switch 1 off. Turn switch 2 on for five minutes and then turn it off. Turn switch 3 on. Enter the room. If a bulb is on, it's controlled by switch 3. Feel the lightbulb for heat. A warm bulb is controlled by switch 2. A bulb that is off and cold is controlled by switch 1.

Solution: Get an additional data point by noting that lightbulbs give off heat.

61 BRICK OVERBOARD

This puzzle tests our understanding of Archimedes' principle. This is almost exactly the problem that Archimedes of Syracuse faced when King Hiero II asked him to determine if a gold crown the king commissioned was pure gold or not.

If you are on a boat and toss a brick overboard, will the water level rise or fall?

Hint: Volume versus displacement.

The brick in the boat displaces an amount of water equal to the *mass* of the brick. The brick in the water displaces an amount of water equal to the *volume* of the brick. Water is unable to support the level of salinity it would take to make it as dense as a brick—the brick will always sink—so the mass is definitely more than the volume. The brick displaces more water when it is in the boat than when it is in the water.

Solution: The water level drops.

62 WHAT COLOR IS THE BEAR?

This is one of the world's best known puzzles. It's hard to imagine it being new to anyone, and once you know the solution, there's not much to it. I include it here only to help set up another puzzle, which can give candidates real heartburn.

A hunter sets up camp, walks 10 miles south and 10 miles east. He shoots a bear and drags it 10 miles north back to his camp. What color is the bear?

Hint: Does anyone really need a hint for this one?

The color of the bear is white because only polar bears live at the North Pole, the location of his camp, the only place on earth where one can walk 10 miles south, 10 miles east, and 10 miles north and be at the starting point. Or are there other such places? We will dig into this question more in the next puzzle.

Solution: White.

Now, let's look at a more generalized form of the previous puzzle. Some candidates are tempted to answer "white" even before the interviewer is finished asking the question. Make sure you listen to the entire question before answering. This one may sound like the previous puzzle, but it's a completely different challenge calling on sophisticated spatial reasoning skills.

How many points are there on the globe where, by walking 10 miles south, 10 miles east, and 10 miles north, you reach the place where you started?

Hint: Think the South Pole neighborhood.

We know that the North Pole is one such place. But it turns out there are an infinite number of points on earth that satisfy the conditions. Here's how one candidate discussed this puzzle:

> Well, the North Pole, for sure. But there are many points in the southern hemisphere as well. There would be a ring of points very near the South Pole such that when you walk 10 miles south, you reach a longitude where the circumference of the ring is exactly 10 miles. In other words, you could start from any point on a circle drawn around the South Pole at a distance slightly more than 10 + ½ pi miles from the Pole. After walking 10 miles south, your next leg of 10 miles east will take you on a complete circumnavigation of the Pole, and the walk 10 miles north from there will return you to the starting point. Thus your starting point could be any one of the infinite points on the latitude with a radius of about 11.59 miles from the South Pole. But if you want even more points, you could also start at locations closer to the Pole, so that the walk east would carry you twice (or three times, or four times!) around the Pole.

Solution: An infinite number of points.

63 SEMICONDUCTOR WAFERS

This brainteaser tests the operations skills of candidates as well as their ability to work with constraints.

In a custom microchip processing plant, workers shape 1 gram packages of silicon semiconductor material into custom microprocessor wafers. During the manufacturing process, not all the silicon is used. For every 5 wafers the plant fabricates, there is enough extra silicon to make 1 additional wafer. Suppose a worker is presented with 25 grams of silicon. What is the maximum number of wafers she can make?

Hint: Reminder of the remainder.

This is a classic remainder problem because the byproducts of the process can be reused. First, the 25 grams of silicon make 25 microchip wafers. This process generates $\frac{25}{5}$ or 5 grams of excess silicon. This extra silicon is used to make 5 additional wafers. While making these 5 additional wafers, 1 additional gram of silicon is generated, which can be used to create 1 more wafer. The maximum number of wafers the plant can fabricate is 25 plus 5 plus 1, or 31 wafers.

Solution: 31 wafers.

Extra credit: Mention that there is ⅕ gram of silicon left over.

64 MOUNTAIN HIKERS

Although this sounds like a probability problem, it really is a logic puzzle, so articulate the logic.

There is a single path up a mountain. A hiker starts hiking up at 6 a.m. and reaches the top at 6 p.m. She stays at the top overnight. She starts down the mountain at 6 a.m. and arrives at the bottom at 6 p.m. On each day, the hiker travels at varying speeds. What are the chances that there was a specific spot on the mountain path that she encountered at exactly the same time of day on both the ascent and the descent?

Hint: Split up the operations and run them concurrently.

With problems like this, it's critical to listen to the statement of the puzzle and especially the challenge. "What are the chances. . . ?" Given the information, this is your clue that the chances are probably either 100 percent, 50 percent, or 0 percent. It's unlikely that a puzzle like this requires a rigorous calculation of probability. More likely, it's either possible or not, and since puzzles are unlikely to be posed if the situation is really impossible (puzzle 51 is an exception to this rule), you have eliminated 0 percent. The real problem, though, is explaining your answer. So the challenge is to think logically and repunctuate the problem. Here's one candidate's logical response:

The answer is 100 percent, and here's how to visualize the proof. Imagine both the hiker's trips taking place simultaneously. That is, the climber starts up at the same time her "twin" starts down. At some point along the way, regardless of whether one hiker stops to tie her shoelaces and the other one doesn't stop at all, they will inevitably encounter each other as they cross paths. They must meet at some point along the path, and at that specific meeting place, they will fulfill the conditions of the puzzle.

Solution: 100 percent chance.

65 MIXED-UP PILLS

Here's a nonmath, process-oriented puzzle that would be especially appropriate for any job that required excellent process or procedural skills.

A patient has fallen very ill and has been advised to take exactly one pill of medicine A and exactly one pill of medicine B each day. The two pills, which are indistinguishable, must be taken together. If they are not, the patient will die. The patient has bottles of A pills and B pills. She puts one of the A pills in her hand. Then while tilting the bottle of B pills, two B pills accidentally fall out. Now there are three pills in her hand. Because all the pills look identical, she cannot tell which two pills are type B and which is type A. Since the pills are extremely expensive, the patient does not wish to throw away the ones in her hand. How can she save the pills in her hand and still maintain a proper daily dosage?

Hint: Take half a pill and call me in the morning.

The key insight required here is that there must be a 1:1 ratio between the active ingredients of A pills and B pills. Don't get hung up about the physical shape that the pills currently have, don't assume the pills have to be manipulated intact, and let go of the assumption that you need to be able to label the pills. There are dozens of solutions. Here are two analyses, both of which have the same effect:

1. Take an extra pill out of the A bottle to make two pills of each type of medication. It is not important to know which is which to know that a 1:1 ratio exists. Now cut each pill in half, being careful to keep the halves separate. For the first night, take half of one pill from each pile and you will be guaranteed exactly one A and one B pill. Save the other halves for tomorrow.

2. Add one A pill to the three pills. The pile now includes two A and two B pills. Again, it is not important to identify which is which. Crush all four pills with a mortar and pestle, making sure the compound is mixed thoroughly. Now take half of the powder today and the rest of the powder the next day. No pill is wasted and the patient gets the right ratio of medication.

66 SHAKING HANDS

This is a nice word puzzle that calls on candidates to conceptualize a process. You don't have to know that this is a well-known problem in combinatorial mathematics called the pigeonhole principle.

Picture the successful candidate for this position. He or she is hired, and there's a big welcome party with 153 fellow employees wanting to shake the candidate's hand. Since a number of people in the room don't know each other, there's a lot of random handshaking among the staff, too. No one can know exactly how many handshakes there were in total. The question is, can we say with certainty that there were at least two people present who shook the exact same number of hands? How can we be sure?

Hint: Think pigeonholes.

Let's start with what we do know. We know that each person could have shaken the hands of any number of people from zero to 152. There were 153 people present but no one shakes hands with himself. One way to conceptualize this puzzle is to distribute the 153 people by putting each one of them into a pigeonhole. The individual who shook hands with 1 person goes into hole 1, the individual who shook hands with 2 people, goes into hole 2, and so on. With 153 people, you can get 153 different pigeonholes filled before anyone has to "share" a pigeonhole.

But what about pigeonhole zero? Is it occupied by someone who didn't shake hands with anyone? If so, then no one can occupy pigeonhole 152. Here's the crux of the puzzle stated another way. If anyone had the number zero, meaning he or she shook no hands, then no one could have the number 152. For that to happen, that person would have had to shake hands with himself. As a result, when you get to the end, when you get to the 153rd person, you say how many hands did you shake? He's got no choice but to repeat a number that's already been used and then has to share that pigeonhole.

Solution: Yes, it is certain that at least 2 people shook the same number of hands.

67 EIGHT BALL—FINDING THE DEFECTIVE BILLIARD BALL

A balance is a simple two-pan setup, like the instrument held by the blindfolded figure of Justice in many courtrooms. It tells you which of the two pans is heavier, though not by how much. It can also tell you when the two pans are of equal weight. This puzzle is known throughout the world, but it still shows up in job interviews.

You have eight billiard balls. One of them is defective in that it weighs more than the others. How do you tell, using a balance, which ball is defective in two weighings?

Hint: You get information by not weighing, too.

The first choice of most candidates—to weigh four balls against four balls—will not work. You will learn that one of four balls is the heavier one, but will need at least two more weighings to isolate the defective ball. The strategy that seems to work best is anarchist thinking. Work through the options, like this candidate does:

I don't think weighing four balls against four balls will work. We would know that the heavier pan contained the defective ball. But when we split the balls in that group into two pairs and weighed the pairs against each other, we would need one more weighing to identify the defective ball. So that's one weighing too many.

Let's leverage the fact that whenever two pans are of equal weight, we can conclude the defective ball is not in either pan. So now for the first weighing let's pick any three balls and weigh them against any other three balls. One outcome is that two pans balance. In that case, the defective ball must be one of the two balls we have set aside. In that case, for the second weighing, all we have to do is compare the two untested balls. The heavier is the defective ball.

The other possible outcome of the first weighing is that the pans do not balance. In that case, the defective ball must be one of the three balls in the heavier pan. For the second weighing, we set aside one ball and weigh the two remaining balls from the heavier pan against each other. If one pan is heavier, it holds the defective ball. If both pans are equal, the defective ball must be the third ball that we set aside.

As far as I know, this is the only two-step solution to this brainteaser. *Solution:* Set aside two balls and weigh three balls against three balls.

68 12 BALLS—FINDING THE DEFECTIVE BILLIARD BALL

This balance beam puzzle has proved to be a favorite at Microsoft. And why not? It's by no means trivial, and yet requires a good deal of mental dexterity. It differs from the previous puzzle in that there are 12 balls, not 8, and now the candidate doesn't know if the defective ball is lighter or heavier than the others.

There are 12 billiard balls of equal size and shape, but one ball is either lighter or heavier than the other 11. Using no more than three balance weighings, can you specify which ball is different and whether it is lighter or heavier?

Hint: Divide and conquer. Divide the problem into simpler steps, and then assemble the simpler steps into a final solution.

Always listen to the phrasing of the question and notice what information is available to you from the phrasing. The same puzzle would be experienced much differently with this phrasing: what is the minimum number of weighings required to specify which ball is different and whether it is lighter or heavier? Here, you are being told that the number of weighings is three and the challenge is to specify the algorithm, or steps, to isolate the unique ball.

There are dozens of approaches to this problem, but only one approach forces a solution in just three weighings. A good way to start is to simplify. Consider 2 balls: 1 blue, 1 red, and the other 10 being white and of the same weight. Balance the red ball against any white ball. If they balance, the blue ball is different, but you still need another balance to determine if it's lighter or heavier.

Now consider 3 balls: 1 blue, 1 red, 1 green, and the 9 others being white and of the same weight. You could balance the blue, red, and green balls against any 3 white balls, which tells you if the different ball is lighter or heavier. You could balance the blue and red balls against any 2 white balls. If they balance, the green ball is different. If they don't balance, you at least know if you're looking for a lighter ball or a heavier ball. If you previously determined either the red, blue, or green ball is heavier, balance the blue ball against the red ball. If they balance, the green ball is heavier. The challenge is now to generalize. Consider how two candidates came at the problem using very different approaches. The first candidate took a traditional narrative approach:

> Since 12 balls contain four groups of 3, and it takes two weighings to determine which group of 3 contains the different ball, the final answer would require four weighings. This suggests that we need to deal with groups of 4 or more to have a chance. Let's begin by balancing two groups of 4. If they balance, the unique ball is among the remaining 4. Now let's select 3 of the remaining 4 to balance against any 3 of the known good balls. If they don't balance, we've at least determined whether we're looking for a lighter or heavier ball.

If the first two groups of 4 do not balance, it's a bit trickier. Let's suppose the left side is heavier. We need to remember that there could be a lighter ball on the right side. For the second weighing, replace 3 balls on the left (heavy) side with 3 balls from the remaining 4, and in addition, swap the fourth ball on the left side with any ball from the right side. If the scale now balances, we know that 1 of the 3 balls removed from the left side is heavier. If the left side is now lighter, 1 of the 2 balls swapped is different. If the right side is still lighter, we know that 1 of the 3 balls on the right side that wasn't swapped is lighter.

The second candidate, obviously a programmer, went up to the whiteboard and solved the problem using his own pseudocode:

find-oddball:

    weigh 4 vs. 4, save 4

    Case match:

    Discard 8 just weighed

Remark: Still have to determine whether it's heavier or lighter

    weigh 3(unknown) vs. 3(known from before), save 1

    Case match:

        Discard 3 just weighed

        weigh 1 vs. 1 known ball

        Case match:

            assert(!"Stated conditions were not met.");

        Case mismatch:

            Tag ball appropriately

            return ball, status

    Case mismatch:

        Tags all remaining balls appropriately lighter/heavier

        weigh 1 vs 1, save 1

        Case match:

            Discard 2 just weighed

return remainder, status.

Case mismatch:

return the one that matches its previously calculated status.

Case mismatch:

Discard 4.

Tags balls WRT which side was lighter/heavier

weigh 3(2 * heavy,light) vs. 3(2 * heavy,light), save 2(heavy,light)

Case match:

Discard 6

weigh either of the remainder vs. any known ball.

Case match:

return the other ball, it's status;

Case mismatch:

return the measured ball, it's status;

Case mismatch:

Remark: It's 1 of the 2 heavies on the heavy side, or the light on the light side

weigh 2 heavies:

Case match:

return light ball from previous step, light

Case mismatch:

return heaviest of the two, heavy

Remark: Test program

struct

ball

hidden_field (Values: normal, heavy, light,)

tag-field-0

tag-field-1

calculated-status

main

ball[12]

ball[random(12)].hidden_field = (random(2) (heavy, light);

oddball = find-oddball(all of the balls)

assert (oddball.calculated-status == oddball.hidden_field)

Solution: Start by balancing two groups of 4 balls.

69 CONTAMINATED PILLS

This puzzle, also a favorite at Microsoft, demonstrates a particularly elegant approach to problem solving that is typical of world-class programmers and analysts.

You have five jars of pills. One jar of pills is contaminated. The only way to tell which pills are contaminated is by weight. A regular pill weighs 10 grams; a contaminated pill weighs 9 grams. You are given a scale and allowed to make just one measurement with it. How do you tell which jar is contaminated?

Hint: Sampling.

This is a classic technical interview puzzle. There really isn't a trick—it is a matter of working through the possible solutions to find one which works. There are possibly some assumptions you have to get out of the way—make sure you've framed the problem correctly—and then the answer emerges. Consider how *The Critical Connection* blog (http://w-uh.com/) analyzes the puzzle:

> You basically have five unknowns—each of the jars could be the one which is contaminated. You are only allowed to perform one weighing, and the answer must discriminate amongst the five unknowns. So how does one weighing give you one of five possibilities? Well, clearly the result of the weighing is a number, so you have to design the experiment so the numeric result tells you what you want to know.

One of the assumptions you have to get through is that weighing the jars themselves is helpful. After a little thought you realize it isn't. Another assumption is that you can only weigh one pill from each jar. This is not a stated constraint, and in fact weighing only one pill from each jar won't get you the answer. The solution is to weigh a different number of pills from each jar. Say you take one pill from jar 1, two from jar 2, three from jar 3, and four from jar 4. (You can take five from jar 5 or more elegantly zero from jar 5, either way you'll get the answer.) Now there are five cases and five possible results:

Jar 1 is contaminated. The weight will be $1 \cdot 9 + 2 \cdot 10 + 3 \cdot 10 + 4 \cdot 10 = 99$

Jar 2 is contaminated. The weight will be $1 \cdot 10 + 2 \cdot 9 + 3 \cdot 10 + 4 \cdot 10 = 98$

Jar 3 is contaminated. The weight will be $1 \cdot 10 + 2 \cdot 10 + 3 \cdot 9 + 4 \cdot 10 = 97$

Jar 4 is contaminated. The weight will be $1 \cdot 10 + 2 \cdot 10 + 3 \cdot 10 + 4 \cdot 9 = 96$

Jar 5 is contaminated. The weight will be $1 \cdot 10 + 2 \cdot 10 + 3 \cdot 10 + 4 \cdot 10 = 100$

Says Ole Eichorn: "This puzzle would be a *pons asinorum* for me, that is, if a programming candidate couldn't figure this out after a while, I'd probably consider them non-qualified." By the way, a *pons asinorum* is a problem that severely tests the ability of an inexperienced person. That phrase is the basis for a puzzle in itself.

For a more conversational approach to this puzzle, consider this candidate's response:

If I'm allowed just one weighing, I need to get all the information necessary to discriminate between contaminated and noncontaminated pills. Here's one way to approach the problem. First, mark the jars with numbers from 1 to 5. Now, take 1 pill from jar 1, take 2 pills from jar 2, take 3 pills from jar 3, take 4 pills from jar 4, and take 5 pills from jar 5. Put all of the 15 selected pills on the scale and take the measurement. Now, if all the pills were noncontaminated, that is each weighed 10 grams, the total weight on the scale would be 150 grams ($1 \cdot 10 + 2 \cdot 10 + 3 \cdot 10 + 4 \cdot 10 + 5 \cdot 10$). But since a number of contaminated pills actually weigh 9 grams, the total will be somewhat less. How much less? Subtract the actual measurement from 150, and the resulting number will point directly to the contaminated jar.

I'm not aware of any other way to solve this problem. By the way, it is easy to demonstrate that this solution works. Assume that jar 4 has the contaminated pills. Then the total weight on the scale will be ($1 \cdot 10 + 2 \cdot 10 + 3 \cdot 10 + 4 \cdot 9 + 5 \cdot 10 = 146$. Now subtract 146 from 150, which leaves 4, the number of the jar containing the contaminated pills.

Solution: Take as many pills from each jar as corresponds to the number of the jar.

70 THREE ANTS IN A TRIANGLE

On one level, this puzzle rewards candidates with a sturdy grasp of probability. But it also requires mental dexterity and may identify candidates with a strong ability to visualize a dynamic situation.

There are three ants at the corners of a regular triangle. Each ant starts moving on a straight line toward another, on a randomly chosen course. What is the probability of avoiding an ant pileup?

Hint: Create a grid of outcomes if you have to.

Here are three different responses from three candidates. Note that while all come to the same answer, their approaches are totally different. Most interviewers agree that the approaches are more important than the answer. Candidate A's response is clearly explained. Candidate B responds with a story, even assigning a name to the ant. Candidate C is clearly the most rigorously educated. Which candidate would you prefer on your team? The important thing is to think out loud so the interviewer can follow your reasoning.

Candidate A: Each ant can move only in two directions. Multiply the number of ants by the number of directions ($2 \cdot 2 \cdot 2 = 8$ ways) to get the total number of possibilities. Now, there are only two ways the ants can avoid running into each other. Either they all travel clockwise, or they all travel counterclockwise. Otherwise, there has to be a collision. Half the possibilities will result in collisions; half will result in no collisions. So the answer is half of 8, or 1 in 4, or 25 percent.

Candidate B: Select one ant and call him "Willie." Once Willie decides which way to go (clockwise or counterclockwise), the other ants have to go in the same direction to avoid a collision. Since the ants choose randomly, there is a 1-in-2 chance the second ant will move in the same direction as Willie, and a 1-in-2 chance the third ant will do the same. That means there is a 1-in-4 chance of avoiding a collision.

Candidate C: Consider the triangle ABC. Let's assume that the ants move toward different corners along the edges of the triangle. The total number of movements is eight ($A \rightarrow B$, $B \rightarrow C$, $C \rightarrow A$ $A \rightarrow B$, $B \rightarrow A$, $C \rightarrow A$ $A \rightarrow B$, $B \rightarrow A$, $C \rightarrow B$ $A \rightarrow B$, $B \rightarrow C$, $C \rightarrow B$ $A \rightarrow C$, $B \rightarrow C$, $C \rightarrow A$ $A \rightarrow C$, $B \rightarrow A$, $C \rightarrow A$ $A \rightarrow C$, $B \rightarrow A$, $C \rightarrow B$ $A \rightarrow C$, $B \rightarrow C$, $C \rightarrow B$). The number of noncolliding movements is two: (2 $A \rightarrow B$, $B \rightarrow C$, $C \rightarrow A$ $A \rightarrow C$, $B \rightarrow A$, $C \rightarrow B$). All ants move in either the clockwise or anti-clockwise direction at the same time. P (not colliding) $= 2/8 = 0.25$.

Solution: One-in-four chance or 25 percent of avoiding a collision.

71 TWO BROTHERS, TWO HORSES

Some versions of this puzzle unnecessarily specify "camels," "sheikhs," and an Arabian Desert setting. Given the daily headlines, from experience I can report that some people will be distracted by such specificity of geography. Better to keep the geography more neutral. But—camels or horses or llamas—it's a classic puzzle and has a highly satisfactory solution.

The time had come when the father of two sons was to decide who would receive his fortune. The father said, "You will both race your horses to the nearest city. The owner of whichever

horse arrives at the gates second will receive my fortune."
Confused, both brothers rode their horses toward the city as
slowly as they could. Outside the gates they loitered for a few
days, neither wanting to be the first to enter the gates. As luck
would have it, a great sage was passing by. Seeing him, the
brothers pleaded for his wisdom. The great sage said two words,
whereupon the brothers quickly mounted and raced as fast as
they could through the gates of the city. What was the great
sage's advice?

Hint: Challenge your assumptions.

The great sage told them to swap horses. It is the second horse, not
the person, to reach the city gates that wins fortune for its owner.

Solution: Trade horses.

72 FIRE ON THE ISLAND

This is an elegant word puzzle that at first appears to be a math problem.
But candidates should quickly understand that something else is being
called for here.

Max is trapped on a heavily forested island that's a narrow
strip of land 10 miles long. A fire has started on the south end
and is moving toward Max at the rate of 1 mile per hour fed
by a wind from the south at 2 miles per hour. What can Max do
to save himself from burning to death? Assume that Max can't
swim and he has no devices of any kind.

Hint: Think backburning.

Solution: Max needs to set a controlled second fire and take advantage of the dead zone that results from the controlled burn. Max doesn't
even need a match or lighter since the current fire is moving slowly
enough that he can get a light from it, bring it a few miles downwind of
the fire, and then start the new fire. Eventually the first fire will reach

the origin of the controlled fire and extinguish itself from lack of fuel. This practice is called "backburning."

Extra credit: Max can jump in the water and drown. It satisfies the challenge since Max does not burn to death.

73 UNCERTAIN CARDS

What is out of sight is often out of mind. Only about 20 percent of people get the right answer to this seemingly simple puzzle because of that truism. This type of puzzle is known as the Wason selection task, named after the psychologist Peter Wason who described it in 1966. The swindle here is that people prefer to reason from sure things. Because people shy away from reasoning about things that are unknown or uncertain, they will select clues that mislead them.

Identify which cards you need to turn over to test the following rule: if there is a vowel on one side of the card, there is an even number on the other side. (See Figure 4.4.)

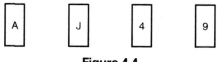

Figure 4.4

Hint: Don't be afraid to reason from uncertainty.

As always, consider the obvious choices and articulate why you reject them. In this case, the two most popular obvious choices are to select just the A card or the A and 4 cards. Let's take these options one at a time because they both have merit. Turning over the A card allows us to test the rule that a vowel on one side (A is a vowel) requires an even number on the other side. If there's an odd number on the other side, the rule has been successfully tested and rejected. But if there is an even number, can we say that the rule has been successfully tested? No, because perhaps some other condition accounts for the even number. Perhaps letters made up of only straight lines is the property associated with even numbers.

If a candidate gets this far, he or she will argue that the A card and the 4 card together can test the rule. That's wrong, too. Four is an even number, and the rule says that if there's a vowel on one side, then there's got to be an even number on the other side. It doesn't say that only vowel cards have even numbers. Say there's a Q on the other side of the 4 card or a picture of a giraffe. It wouldn't disprove the rule. Whether there's a vowel or a consonant or something else, it makes no difference. The 4 card is irrelevant.

Actually, you need two cards: the A card *and* the 9 card. Why? The 9 card represents a key test of the rule because if there is a vowel on the other side of the 9, it disproves the rule.

Because the A card is the only vowel card and the 4 is the only even-number card, it is tempting for candidates to jump to the faulty conclusion that they should turn over the 4. The better strategy is to push one's mind to reason from uncertainty. You know (or hope) there's a letter—vowel or consonant—behind the 9 card, but you can't see it so you downplay its significance. The technical term for this is disjunction: an either-or situation where exactly one of the two or more mutually exclusive outcomes is true. When a problem presents a disjunction, the trick is to list all the possibilities and reason from each of them. "What if the unseen letter is a vowel. . . ? What if the unseen letter is a consonant. . . ?

74 PRISONER AND CIGARETTE

This is a thought experiment about power. There is no right or wrong answer. The puzzle explores the limits of power that a seemingly powerless person controls. This puzzle was the subject of a contest on my Web site in which dozens of people submitted entries. Some of the most creative submissions are below, followed by the answer I think most elegant.

You are a prisoner in solitary confinement serving a life sentence without possibility of parole. It is Friday afternoon, and you absolutely must have a cigarette. The only person who

can give you one is the guard outside your cell. What do you do to get a cigarette?

Hint: This is not a trick question. Any prisoner in the world can try it today.

Thanks to all the contestants for sending in entries. Unfortunately, the volume of responses makes it impossible to include them all in this book. (See additional entries on my Web site: www.jkador.com). The first runner-up, Maximilien Poux of Merrill Lynch Capital Markets in France, has a refreshing health-based solution:

> I would call the guard and tell him that if he gives me a cigarette, he'll live six minutes longer, and I'll live six minutes less. This fact being proven scientifically, I'll swap with him my useless and painful minutes in prison, so that he can enjoy his life longer. . . . And, since I'm sentenced to spend my life in jail, by having me dead sooner (other things being equal), he'll have less work to do, and more time to live! Therefore it's a good deal for both of us! . . .

Second runner-up Lorie Pomeroy of Austin, Texas, suggests the inmate can earn a cigarette by performing a service:

> Basically I would identify a need/desire the guard has and determine a way that I can fulfill that need/desire and earn the cigarette. I could write a love poem for his significant other, draft a letter to a credit card company regarding an erroneous charge or any number of correspondences that he/she may need. Or I could earn the cigarette by providing entertainment to him, such as singing, telling jokes, creating and telling short stories.

The third runner-up, Martin Sweitzer, had a powerful suggestion in the first part of his answer, but then he threw it away to pursue a course that to my mind is a lot weaker:

> I would get the guard's attention. Tapping on the door. Pounding. Saying I am going to commit suicide on his watch. Once I have his attention I point out how much better he really is than the other guards and that he certainly should get a promotion. Then I would say that for a cigarette, I will fake a daring escape and he can be

the guard to single-handedly capture me, gaining the respect of his peers and the acknowledgment of his supervisor.

Sweitzer actually anticipates the answer that I think is strongest. First, let's look at the puzzle again. What's the most curious part of the clue? If you guessed "Friday afternoon," you are right. What does Friday afternoon matter to an inmate serving a life sentence? It doesn't. But it matters to the guard, who presumably values his weekend. My solution accounts for all the clues. The prisoner says to the guard:

> Listen, I need one cigarette. I know you don't have to give me one, but if you don't, I will try to commit suicide right now. Maybe I'll succeed and maybe I won't, but in any case I'll be injured, and you'll have to send me to the morgue or the infirmary. You'll have mountains of paperwork to fill out, and you'll be here for hours cutting into your weekend. Please give me just one cigarette, and I'll be good until your shift is over and I'm someone else's problem.

Now the response from Alik Gotlib, the winner of the contest, which is so psychologically astute that it just might get a bored guard to play along. I like the solution because it swindles the cigarette from the guard. Gotlib, a senior software developer at Matrix Software in Israel, receives a signed copy of this book as his prize:

> Usually the jail guards are extremely bored, just like the prisoners. So they would be glad to have any entertainment, especially if it is not very sophisticated and intellectual. So the prisoner may start an easy conversation with the guard, tell him some jokes, and after that he may ask: "Hey, man, do you know why they call me Jack-two-cigarettes? Because my penis is exactly 19 cm long! That is exactly the length of two cigarettes! Wanna check it out?"
>
> The guard would be intrigued. He might say "Prove it!" and throw me two cigarettes. I would then place the cigarettes along my penis and say in surprise, "Not even close. You win!" Or perhaps I'd say, "Hah! Perfect match!" In any case, the guard will not want his cigarettes back. So the guard will have a laugh, and I will have not one, but two cigarettes.

REASONING PUZZLES THAT REQUIRE MATH

These puzzles all require some application of mathematics. Most of the problems require little more than simple arithmetic. A few call for geometry and elementary algebra. None require calculus or anything close to it. Remember, if you find yourself calculating a sum of a series or integrating a differential, you are probably way off base. These puzzles are never about testing math skills. There are better ways to do that, and if you are applying to be an actuary, for example, your skills will be tested in other ways. These puzzles are not part of that test. Rather, these puzzles call on a variety of cognitive skills that happen to be easily represented mathematically. The puzzles are presented from least to most challenging.

75 SNAIL IN A WELL

This puzzle has been vetted for simplicity because it is included in virtually every puzzle book for children. Sometimes the protagonist is an earthworm or a frog. The puzzle is included here only because a candidate who offers the obvious wrong answer may indicate intellectual laziness.

A snail is at the bottom of a well that is 20 feet in depth. Every day the snail climbs 5 feet upward, but at night it slides 4 feet back down. After how many days can the snail climb out of the well?

Hint: Spring forward, fall back.

Watch out! This is a classic trap. The obvious answer is to reason that since the snail nets 1 foot per day in its climb, it will work its way out of the 20-foot well after 20 days. Duh! The only thing that you need to do here is take your time and work the puzzle out day by day. In fact, the snail is not moving at 1 foot per day but moving up 5 then falling 4. This means that on day 1, it is up to 5 and then down to 1. Day 2 it is up to 6 and then down to 2. Day 3 it is up to 7 and down to 3. On the sixteenth day the happy snail will go up to 20 and not go down any more (because he is out of there!).

Solution: 16 days.

76 VALUE BETWEEN 4 AND 5

This problem was recently featured on the Car Talk *Puzzler. It's a good puzzle for job interviews over meals because cocktail napkins serve very well for drawing out the puzzle. It's difficult because it's so simple. Most people get it with a little hint. The interviewer takes a piece of paper and writes the number "4," leaving a little space, and then writes the number "5" (see Figure 5.1).*

What common mathematical symbol, when placed between the numbers 4 and 5, will result in a number that is greater than 4 but less than 6?

4 5

Figure 5.1

Hint: Mathematical symbols don't have to be operators.

Further hint: It's a common mathematical symbol that's used every day, including on the restaurant menu.

Solution: Place a decimal point between the 4 and 5, resulting in the value 4.5.

77 LIGHT BEER, DARK BEER

This is a fun puzzle that interviewers have been known to trot out at job interviews conducted over meals.

A man goes into a bar and places a dollar bill on the counter. "Glass of beer, please," he says to the bartender.

The bartender asks, "Light or dark?"

"What's the difference in price?" says the man.

"Light beer is $0.90, dark beer is $1.00," replies the bartender.

"Okay, I'll have the dark beer," says the man.

Then another man comes into the bar and places $1.00 on the bar. "Glass of beer, please," says the second man. The bartender without a word gives him a dark beer.

How did the bartender know what kind of beer the second man wanted?

Hint: Change the parameters.

There's not much to this puzzle except that most people make an assumption that when the second man placed $1 on the bar, he was using paper money. Maybe there are other solutions to this puzzle, but none are as satisfying as this recruiter's favorite response:

> The first man placed a dollar bill on the counter. The second man placed a dollar in coins on the counter. The coins consisted of three quarters, two dimes, and a nickel. Unlike the first man, the second customer had exact change for the $0.90 light beer. The bartender knew that the customer understood the pricing. Since the customer put down $1.00, the bartender concluded that the customer in fact ordered the dark beer.

Solution: The man paid with coins.

78 COUNTERFEIT BILL

On one level, this puzzle is so simple it would be laughed at by any high school economics class. So why do so many sophisticated businesspeople get perplexed by it?

A customer buys a widget from a vendor for $3. The customer gives the vendor a $10 bill. The vendor does not usually deal with cash, so he goes to the business next door to get change. The vendor then gives the customer the widget and $7 in change. After the customer leaves, the business next door determines that the $10 bill is counterfeit. Embarrassed, the vendor gives the neighboring business a genuine $10 bill from his wallet. How much value has the vendor lost in the transaction?

Hint: What does the vendor have left?

There is only one relevant transaction. The salient feature of this transaction is that in exchange for a worthless piece of paper, the vendor gave up $7 plus the widget. The $3 change that the vendor received is the only thing of value he gets to keep.

Solution: $7 plus the widget.

79 BUMBLEBEE TRAIN

At first it not only seems that this problem requires math to solve, but that it requires calculus. When a problem like this (and the next one) seems too hard to solve, you know that there's an out-of-the-box trick and your real puzzle is to reframe the problem. After that it will be easy.

Two trains enter a tunnel 200 miles long traveling at 100 miles per hour toward each other from opposite directions. As soon as they enter the tunnel, a supersonic bumblebee flying at 1,000 miles per hour starts from one train and heads toward the other one. As soon as it reaches the second locomotive, it reverses course and heads back toward the first, going back and forth between the rapidly approaching trains until the trains collide in a fiery explosion in the middle of the tunnel. How far does the bee travel until it meets its untimely end?

Hint: How much time is the bee in transit?

Think about this problem a minute. At first blush, this is an infinite-series problem. And while college math majors can possibly sum up an infinite series like this, it's highly improbable that an interviewer will want you to do so. So there's got to be a shortcut or trick. Your job is to find the "aha!" insight, like this candidate did:

> On first hearing, my heart sank because I thought this problem requires calculus. I can do the integral to sum up the ever-decreasing distances that the bee travels, but maybe there's another way . . . let's simplify. The tunnel is 200 miles long. The trains meet in the middle traveling at 100 miles per hour. That means the trains collide in one hour. The bee is traveling at 1,000 miles per hour for one hour before the trains collide. So, assuming that the bee reverses course without losing speed, I guess it travels 1,000 miles before the trains meet.

Solution: 1,000 miles.

80 26 CONSTANTS

Okay, don't panic. When faced with a puzzle of this difficulty, there is always a shortcut or trick. Relax your mind and forget about integral calculus. Don't even go there. There's a way out of this thicket. Finding it is the puzzle.

You have 26 constants, labeled A through Z. Let A equal 1. The other constants have values equal to the letter's position in the alphabet, raised to the power of the previous constant. In other words, B *(the second letter)* = $2^A = 2^1 = 2$, C = $3^B = 3^2 = 9$, and so on. Find the exact numerical value for this expression:

$$(X - A) \cdot (X - B) \cdot (X - C) \cdot \ldots (X - Y) \cdot (X - Z)$$

Hint: What's hidden in the ellipses?

Just looking at this equation makes most people wince. But relax. Solving for the value of *X*, the twenty-fourth letter of the alphabet, calls for a number larger than all the atoms in the universe. Listen to the question. Did you hear the word *exact*? That's your first clue that the value is a simple number. This is one of those trick questions that can be dispatched with a quick "aha!" In puzzles like this, you should always look at the part of the puzzle that's hidden. In this case, that's in the ellipses. If you take a minute and mentally repunctuate that area, you'll soon come to the expression $(X - X)$, which is conveniently zero. An ideal response goes like this:

> The sums from A to W are irrelevant since at X, $(X - X)$, the product will result in zero. Anything multiplied by zero results in an answer of zero. Since one of the terms will be $(X - X)$, which is zero, the entire answer will result in an answer of zero.

Solution: Zero

81 MEASURING 4 QUARTS

This is another very well known puzzle. The quantities of the buckets may change, but the solutions are of the same order. This puzzle challenged Bruce Willis in the movie Die Hard with a Vengeance.

You have a 3-quart bucket, a 5-quart bucket, and an infinite supply of water. How can you measure out exactly 4 quarts?

There are a number of elegant ways to solve this puzzle. Most interviewers will favor the solution with the fewest number of steps.

Optimum Solution

1. Fill the 3-quart bucket and pour into the 5-quart bucket.
2. Again, fill the 3-quart bucket and pour into the 5-quart bucket to the brim. That leaves 1 quart remaining in the 3-quart bucket.
3. Empty the 5-quart bucket.
4. Pour the 1 quart into the 5-quart bucket.
5. Fill the 3-quart bucket again and add it to the 1 quart to make 4 quarts.

Alternative Solution

1. Fill the 5-quart bucket to the brim.
2. Pour the contents into the empty 3-quart bucket until it is full. Now there are 2 quarts in the 5-quart bucket.
3. Empty the 3-quart bucket.

4. Pour the 2 quarts from the 5-quart bucket into the 3-quart bucket.

5. Refill the 5-quart bucket.

6. Fill the 3-quart bucket with 1 quart, leaving 4 quarts in the 5-quart bucket.

Creative Solution

1. Fill 5-quart bucket and pour 3 quarts of water into 3-quart bucket, leaving 2 quarts in 5-quart bucket.

2. Refill the 5-quart bucket.

3. Carefully submerge the 3-quart bucket (now containing 2 quarts of water) into the 5-quart bucket to the brim of the smaller bucket. Now 3 quarts of water from the larger bucket are displaced. Now 2 quarts remain in the 5-quart bucket.

4. Remove the smaller bucket and transfer its 2 quarts into the 5-quart bucket with its 2 quarts.

Xi Ye, a student at the Illinois Mathematics and Science Academy in Aurora, Illinois, objects to the creative solution on the following grounds: "When you submerge the 3-quart bucket into the 5-quart bucket, the volume of the 3-quart bucket would count in the volume of the water displaced from the larger bucket," he says. Xi Ye reminds us that unless the interviewer specifies a bucket without physical mass, creative solutions often bump up against reality.

82 100-METER RACE

A deceptive puzzle reminiscent of the fable about the hare and turtle.

Jack and Jill are in a 100-meter race. When Jill crossed the finish line, Jack was only at the 90-meter mark. Jill suggested they run another race. This time, Jill would start 10 meters behind the starting line. All other things being equal, will Jack win, will Jill win, or will it be a tie?

Jack will lose again. In the second race, Jill started 10 meters back. By the time Jack reaches the 90-meter mark, Jill will have caught up to him.

Therefore, the final 10 meters will belong to the faster of the two. Since Jill is faster than Jack, she will win the final 10 meters and, of course, the race.

Solution: Jill wins the 100-meter race again.

83 EIGHT LOAVES OF BREAD

Here is a puzzle that, while not overly complicated, requires competency with fractions and some insight about resource allocation, profit distribution, and fairness. The puzzle is used in interviews at Hewlett-Packard.

Bob and Dave sit down to eat some bread. Bob has 3 loaves and Dave has 5 loaves. A stranger comes up to them and says that he will pay them if he can share their bread because he is very hungry. They all share the bread equally, and the stranger is very thankful. He says that he has eight coins of equal value to divide between the two men, but he does not know how to divide them.

Bob suggests that he and Dave split the reward equally, with each receiving four coins. Dave disagrees, arguing that the 8 loaves be valued one coin each. Dave insists that since he contributed 5 loaves, it's fair that he get five coins while Bob get three coins. What is the fairest solution to this problem?

Hint: Pay attention to starting conditions. What happens to the bread?

The key insight to the solution of this puzzle is that Bob and Dave do not sell all their bread to the stranger: they retain ⅔ of the bread for themselves. As a result, it is not fair that the stranger pay for the bread that Bob and Ray consume. Candidates who do not acknowledge this distinction miss a key point about resource allocation: profits should equitably go in proportion to the resources invested or risks accepted. When this key point is accepted, the somewhat surprising solution makes sense. A recruiter for Hewlett-Packard who uses this puzzle finds this candidate's response ideal:

There are three people eating the bread, and there are 8 loaves. Each person gets an equal share of the 8 loaves. That means each person receives ⅜ or 2⅔ loaves of bread. So let's see what each person contributes. The hungry stranger contributes eight coins. Bob contributes 3 loaves, but he consumes 2⅔ loaves; therefore, he only gives up ⅓ of 1 loaf to the stranger. Dave contributes 5 loaves, but he consumes 2⅔ loaves; therefore, he gives up 2⅓ of his loaves to the stranger. Dave gives up seven times more bread than Bob. Given the ratio of resources each "sold" to the stranger, the fairest solution is for Bob to get one coin and Dave to get seven coins.

Solution: Bob, the man who contributes 3 loaves, gets one coin; Dave, the man who contributes 5 loaves, gets seven coins.

84 SWIMMING WITH THE TIDE

Some interviewers invite candidates to go up to the whiteboard to reason this puzzle out.

A world-class swimmer can swim at twice the speed of the prevailing tide. She swims out to a buoy and back again, taking four minutes to make the round-trip. How long would it take her to make the identical swim in still water?

While this puzzle can be done with algebra, here's a candidate who figured it out logically:

We know that she swims at twice the speed of the tide. That means that when swimming against the tide, her speed is equal to that of the prevailing tide. In still water, then, she swims at twice the speed of the tide. If we call the time it takes to swim the distance between the shore and buoy 1 splash, then with the tide it will take one-third splash and in still water one-half splash. To swim there and back, then, takes 1 splash in still water and four-thirds splash when there is a tide (since it takes 1 splash for the part of the swim that is against the tide and one-third splash for the part of the swim that is with the tide). This is one-third as long again as the time taken to do the round-trip in still water. Since it takes four minutes when there is a tide, it must take three minutes when there is no tide.

Solution: Three minutes.

85 CANDY INTO THREE PILES

A very clean puzzle that calls on an understanding of factors.

A box of candy can be divided equally (without cutting pieces) among two, three, or seven people. What is the least number of pieces of candy the box could contain?

Hint: Factors.

Discussion: What's the smallest number that has the factors 2, 3, and 7? While there are algebraic ways to solve this problem, the easiest way is by inspection and trial and error.

Solution: 42 pieces of candy.

86 TOURNAMENT MATCHES

This puzzle has "shortcut" written all over it.

You have volunteered to be the chief organizer for the world's table tennis championships. There are 657 contestants from around the world. The tournament is organized as a single elimination, whereby the winner of each match advances and the loser is eliminated. Since there is an odd number of participants, the strongest player gets a bye and automatically advances to the next round. How many matches will the tournament need in order to determine the table tennis champion?

Hint: Think losers, not winners.

Whenever you see a puzzle with a number such as "657" you know you are in the realm of a thought puzzle. Don't even bother taking out a notebook or calculator. This is a thought puzzle, so think. Here's one candidate's response:

Okay, how many competitors are there? 656. Now, for every winner there's a loser. What we are trying to determine is the number of matches needed to come up with 656 *losers*. And how are losers determined? By a match. So there must be a one-to-one correspondence between the number of losers and the number of matches. And 656 losers require 656 matches.

Solution: 656 matches will be needed.

87 BURNING FUSES

A familiar concept for puzzlers is fuses or candles that burn for a specified number of minutes, and the challenge is to use the materials to time a specified interval. Hourglass problems require similar reasoning. The next two puzzles offer a representative sample of this genre.

You have two rope fuses of the type used to ignite explosives. The fuses each take one hour to burn completely. The problem is the fuses are nonuniform and can't be assumed to burn evenly. Using these two fuses and nothing else, how would you time 45 minutes?

Hint: Work with both ends of the fuses.

The obvious (and wrong) approach is to cut the fuses, assuming that half of a one-hour fuse will burn for 30 minutes. If they could, one of the fuses could be cut in half (30 minutes) and the remaining fuse cut in half again (15 minutes), making this a very trivial problem, indeed. If you still think that's a viable approach, you didn't listen to the problem. The implication is that since the fuses are nonuniform, they cannot be cut. Besides not being given a cutting tool, the candidate is forced to find another way. This is how one candidate put it together:

> I'd start by simultaneously lighting both ends of fuse 1 and one end of fuse 2. When fuse 1 is completely burned, 30 minutes will have passed. At that point, I would immediately light the other end of fuse 2. The half-hour strand of fuse 2 will burn in 15 minutes. Thus, I will have determined an elapsed time of 30 minutes plus 15 minutes, or 45 minutes.

Solution: Light both ends of the fuse . . .

88 TWO HOURGLASSES

Another variation of the interval timing problem, this one using hourglasses instead of fuses.

You have two hourglasses. The first one times exactly 7 minutes; the other times exactly 11 minutes. Using just these two hourglasses and nothing else, how would you accurately time 15 minutes?

Hint: Work with both hourglasses at the same time.

The most elegant answer is the quickest. Check out this candidate's response:

> Start both hourglasses at the same time. At the end of 7 minutes, flip over the 7-minute hourglass. In another 4 minutes, the 11-minute hourglass will be empty and 4 minutes will have elapsed from the 7-minute-hourglass. Flip the 7-minute hourglass over and watch the remaining 4 minutes fall away. 7 + 4 + 4 = 15.

Solution: Start both hourglasses simultaneously.

89 WHAT'S THE AVERAGE SALARY?—TAKE ONE

This is an example of a puzzle that tests a candidate's ability to generate and articulate a generalized solution to a problem.

While waiting for their manager to start a meeting, a group of seven employees are discussing salaries. Although company policy prohibits the divulging of individual salaries, the employees agree that it would be useful if they knew the average salary of the group. What strategy will allow them to determine the average salary of the group without anybody knowing the individual salaries of anybody else?

Hint: Disaggregate salary numbers.

This puzzle calls for an awareness that a team can cooperate by compartmentalizing the problem. It also helps to have a good understanding of the concept of averages. A programming background doesn't hurt, because the solution calls for nothing less than a simple routine. Here's one candidate's solution:

> The challenge is to design a generalized solution that yields a group average but protects individual salaries. The first employee makes up a number and whispers it to the second employee. The second employee silently adds her salary to that random number and whispers the new total to the third. The third adds his salary to this and whispers the sum to the fourth. Similarly, the fourth whispers to the fifth, the fifth to the sixth, and the sixth to the seventh. The seventh adds his salary and whispers the resulting sum to the first. The first employee then subtracts the original made-up number, adds her own salary to the total, and then divides by 7 and announces the total.

Alternatively, the first employee can simply announce the group total and leave the division calculation to each employee. Another candidate took a different tack:

> Each employee arbitrarily divides his salary into two component numbers, the sum of which equals his salary. He then gives the first of those numbers to the employee on his left and gives the second one of the numbers to the employee on his right. Thereafter, each employee is responsible for the sum of the left and right (excluding own salary). Each employee, in turn, announces the sum. The sum of all numbers is taken and divided by 7. There is no reason to whisper.

90 CUP OF COFFEE AND TEA

I warn you, this puzzle often arouses passionate arguments. For some reason, people quickly hold tight to the conclusions they reach. In the wrong hands, this puzzle can easily lead to a meltdown of the interview.

You have two identical cups, one filled with coffee and one filled with tea. Take one tablespoon of the coffee and mix it in with

the tea. Now take one tablespoon of this resulting tea-coffee mixture and transfer it back to the cup of pure coffee. Is there more coffee in the cup of tea or more tea in the cup of coffee?

When she posed this puzzle in *Parade Magazine*, Marilyn vos Savant received hundreds of irate letters from mathematicians protesting her solution. People from around the world posted solutions on puzzle Web sites. These correspondents could not accept the answer that there is exactly as much coffee in the tea as there is tea in the coffee. Before we consider the correct arguments, it is useful to review a few of the incorrect ones because they seem very persuasive. A puzzler named Ashutosh writes:

> What the puzzle asks for is to determine the contents of tea and coffee in each cup after one round of transfer (tea into coffee cup and coffee into tea cup). Let's say both cups contain x parts of tea and x parts of coffee. Now I take 1 spoonful of tea and put it into the coffee cup. It forms a mixture of tea and coffee in the coffee cup. Now I take a spoonful of the mixture and put it back into the tea cup. As a result the contents of the tea cup now contain both tea and coffee. It means the coffee cup would contain a little more of its original content as the mixture which was removed from the coffee cup would certainly contain a little less pure coffee (as it would also contain some tea). In short the tea cup loses x parts of pure tea, the coffee cup in turn loses $x - y$ parts of coffee. There is more coffee in the tea cup than tea in the coffee cup.

Another Internet puzzler named Ozzy actually tries to work out the math to support his view that the two cups are not equal:

> Let's say the cups are 100 ounces each and a tablespoon is 10 ounces. When you take 10 ounces of tea and mix it with the coffee, you have 100 ounces coffee and 10 ounces tea. Once evenly mixed, total contents are 110 ounces. Now, for every 10 ounces of coffee there is 1 ounce of tea, which makes the coffee/tea ratio 10/1. So if you add a 10-ounce sample of this mixture back into the tea, you are adding approximately 9.011111111 coffee/.999999999 tea. Now add this mixture back to the tea. In the tea cup, you will have 90.999999999

tea and 9.011111111 coffee, which means for every 9.09 ounces of tea you have .901 ounces of coffee, making your ratio 9.09 tea/.901 coffee, while the coffee cup is still 10/1. When you add it all up, the tea cup ends up with more of its original content.

In fact, the percentages of coffee and tea in the two cups that are of equal volume must be the same. In her book, *The Power of Logical Thinking* (St. Martin's Press, 1966), Marilyn vos Savant explains:

> If cup A contains a certain amount of one liquid, and cup B contains the same amount of another liquid, no matter how many times you transfer the liquids back and forth, or even whether you mix them well or not at all, as long as each cup ends with an equal volume, there will be as much B liquid in cup A as there will be A liquid in cup B. This is because however much B liquid is now in cup A, it displaces the same amount of A liquid, which we will find (where else?) in cup B.

Puzzler Eric Bentley agrees and offers a compelling analogy:

> Here is another way to explain the coffee and tea problem: Take 200 pennies and divide them into piles of 100 heads and 100 tails. Put 10 heads into the 100 tails pile. Now take ANY ten pennies from the 110 combination pile and put them back into the heads pile. For the heads pile you now have 90 heads plus any more heads which you brought back from the combination pile, plus any tails from the combination pile for a total of 100 pennies. The second pile will have the exact opposite composition.

Getting back to liquids, here is Mikael's take on the puzzle:

> This is an easy explanation for the tea and coffee problem that so many people are finding hard to understand: you start with the same amount of tea and coffee in each cup, no matter how much or how many times you mix them, as long as you end up with the same volume in each cup, you will always end up with a percentage of tea in one cup equal to the percentage of coffee in the other. Let's say you have 85 percent tea and 15 percent coffee in your original tea cup; that means, the other 15 percent tea and 85 percent

coffee has to be in the other cup. You don't need a bunch of variables and formulas for this one, just some common sense!

Solution: There is as much coffee in the tea cup as tea in the coffee cup.

91 MARCHING DOG

This is a simple problem suitable for a candidate who has displayed aptitude for algebra.

A marching band is parading down Main Street at a constant speed. The bass drum player has a dog that runs to the front row and then back to its owner, going back and forth, also at a constant speed. The distance between the back row and front row of the marching band is 50 feet. In the time the dog went back and forth, the bass drum player marched 50 feet. Find the length of the dog's path.

While this can be done with a little hit or miss arithmetic, algebra makes it easier:

While the band went x feet ahead, the dog ran $50 + x$

While the band went $50 - x$ dog ran x

So $x/(50 + x) = (50 - x)/x$

$x \cdot x = (50 - x) \cdot (50 + x)$

$x \cdot x = 2{,}500 - x \cdot x$

$2x \cdot x = 2{,}500$

$x = 35$

Solution: 35 feet.

92 FOUR PEOPLE ON A BRIDGE

Candidates report that this problem shows up at many Microsoft job interviews. Its solution requires an elegance of thought, the formation of an algorithm, and a demonstrated ability to juggle three or four things at once. Almost everyone will need a paper or pen to solve this. Some interviewers draw out the puzzle on a whiteboard and invite the candidate to stand up and solve it.

Four programmers must cross a rickety bridge at night. The bridge can only hold two of them at a time, and they have one flashlight between them. The four programmers cross at different speeds: Alex requires one minute, Sam requires two, Pat requires four, and Francis requires eight. What is the shortest time in which they can all cross?

Hint: Get the two slowest people across first.

First, assume that it's, in fact, possible. I've never known an interviewer to present a problem like this and watch the candidate grapple with it, only to say, "Actually, it's not possible." Now the solution to this problem is counterintuitive. For some reason, most people want to get the *fastest* people across first.

The most obvious solution that occurs to most people after working on this problem for a bit is as follows:

Alex + Sam → far side (2 minutes)

Alex → near side (1 minute, total = 3 minutes)

Alex + Pat → far side (4 minutes, total = 7 minutes)

Alex → near side (1 minute, total = 8 minutes)

Alex + Francis → far side (8 minutes, total = 16 minutes)

This is a good solution because it uses Alex to ferry the flashlight back after each trip. Alex is the fastest, so this seems to make sense. Sam, Pat, and Francis each need to cross the bridge, so that's 2 + 4 + 8 = 14 minutes, and Alex has to come back twice, so that's 2 more minutes for a total of 16. How could that not be optimal?

Ole Eichorn, who has administered this puzzle to dozens of job candidates, analyzes the solution set at length on his blog *The Critical Connection* (http://w-uh.com/):

After giving a suboptimal answer to this problem, many people refuse to believe it is wrong. I love this problem for exactly this reason. If candidates work it out by themselves, terrific, they get full credit, but if they get the good-but-wrong answer and accept that it is wrong, and continue digging, I give them full credit for that, too. (There is a bit of an "aha!" involved.) Sometimes people don't believe there's a better answer, and start to argue with you; that's a bad sign; it is good to have confidence, but not good to be closed to new ideas.

So, how could this be done any better? Let's come back to Eichorn:

The optimal answer to this question is actually 15. (Yep, it is, I'll tell you how in a moment.) Now if you were to ask: "How can the four programmers cross in 15 minutes," you may very well stump candidates. This isn't what you want. Ideally you want candidates to chew on the problem, work out a solution, and then defend it. This gives you a lot more insight into how candidates think, and they have a sense of accomplishment. Otherwise if they fail to get 15, they'll feel bad, and you'll feel like you tricked them.

The key insight—the thing which is a bit of an "aha!"—is to have Francis and Pat cross at the same time. They're the two slowest, so essentially this gives you the second-slowest crossing for free. It isn't obvious how to make this happen, though; here's the most likely first attempt:

Francis + Pat → far side (8 minutes)

Pat → near side (4 minutes, total = 12 minutes, already something seems wrong)

Pat + Alex → far side (4 minutes, total = 16 minutes, you know this won't work . . .)

Pat had to come back with the flashlight. This made his 4 minutes far from free, because not only does he have to come back, he has to cross again. Not good. So what if Pat didn't have to come back? What if a faster programmer were already on the far side and could bring the flashlight back instead? Aha!

Alex + Sam → far side (2 minutes)

Alex → near side (1 minute, total = 3 minutes)

Francis + Pat → far side (8 minutes, total = 11 minutes)

Sam → near side (2 minutes, total = 13 minutes, this is the key!)

Sam + Alex → far side (2 minutes, total = 15 minutes)

Excellent, eh? And yet it is quite logical. An exhaustive analysis of all the possibilities in a relatively small solution space would find this easily.

Extra credit: Challenging another assumption yields another "aha!" moment that cuts minutes off the solution thought optimum. The insight—attributed to Ben Webman—is why assume that the illumination provided by the flashlight (the flashlight's "carry") is so poor that it can serve only the person holding it? Why not assume that the flashlight can illuminate part or even all of the bridge. In that case, it might not have to be carried at all. In Webman's response, the flashlight's beam carries all the way, and there's no need to go back with it. For example, let's assume the flashlight's beam carries halfway. Now what's the best solution? Let's first see what this does to the original solution:

Alex + Sam → far side (2 minutes); Alex only goes halfway

Alex → near side (½ minute, total = 3 minutes)

Francis + Pat → far side (8 minutes, total = 10½ minutes)

Sam → middle of bridge (1 minute, total = 11½ minutes, this is the key!)

Sam + Alex → far side (1 minute, total = 12½ minutes)

So the total time is reduced from 15 minutes to 12½ minutes.

Ole Eichorn comments:

How about that! With 100 percent carry, all the programmers can cross in the time it takes Francis to cross the bridge by himself, with only two on the bridge at any one time. That is optimal. (In fact, the carry need only be ⅞ for the same solution.) "How can we be sure 10 minutes is really optimal? We do what all nerds do, we write a program! In such a small solution space it is possible to stochastically examine all possible combinations of movement, seeking a minimum. I did this—modeling the flashlight beam is a little tricky—and sure enough the 10 minute solution for 50 percent carry is optimal.

[To see Eichorn's code, go to http://w-uh.com/images/ progbridge.cpp.txt.]

93 A BALANCING ACT

This puzzle actually requires a good understanding of the physics of seesaws and a willingness to do a calculation. Many engineers are delighted with this puzzle and find its solution very satisfying. The puzzle was featured on the Car Talk *Puzzler, where it was attributed to Tom Fite.*

Consider a seesaw (see Figure 5.2). The board of the seesaw is 1 foot wide and 8 feet long and weighs 36 pounds. But instead of the fulcrum being in the center of the board like a traditional teeter-totter, this fulcrum is actually 2 feet from one end and 6 feet from the other end. On the short side, there is a 1-foot by 1-foot 48-pound weight right at the end of the board. The problem is, what weight do you need on the other side of the board to balance the seesaw?

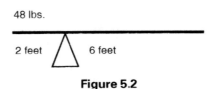

Figure 5.2

Hint: What's the unstated assumption in the problem?

The first thing to note is that the board has weight and must be considered in the weight and balance equation. The 8-foot board weighs 36 pounds, so each foot of board weighs 4.5 pounds. That means on the 2-foot side of the fulcrum, the board weighs 9 pounds; on the 6-foot side, it weighs 27 pounds. The fact that 9 and 27 add up to 36 is good for solving the puzzle.

Now it really helps here to understand something of the physics of seesaws. A seesaw balances when the torque on both sides of the fulcrum is equal. Consider the torque on the 6-foot side of the fulcrum. The center of the mass of the board is at 3 feet (half the length). To calculate the torque of a seesaw, multiply the weight of the board by the feet from the center of mass. In this case, on the right side of the fulcrum it is 27 pounds · 3 feet = 81 pound feet. And that's without an additional weight on it.

Now consider the other side. On the 2-foot side of the fulcrum, there is a 2-foot section that weighs 9 pounds, but that 2-foot section has a center of mass that is 1 foot from the fulcrum. So that piece of board by itself has a torque of 9 · 1, or 9 pound feet. Now the block weighs 48 pounds. Its center of gravity is a foot and a half from the fulcrum. So it's 48 times a foot and a half, which comes out to be 72 pound feet. Adding the weight of the block (72 pound feet) plus the weight of the board (9 pound feet) makes 81 pound feet, exactly the torque of the other side. There is no need to add any weight. The seesaw is perfectly balanced as it is.

Solution: The seesaw is already in balance.

94 BOWLING BALL DROP

This puzzle usually delights software testers who have to "break" software to improve it. The puzzle requires a deep understanding of breaking a complex problem down into manageable steps.

Your job is bowling ball tester. You have two identical bowling balls. Given a 100-story building, your challenge is to figure out from which floor a dropped bowling ball will

shatter on the ground. You know nothing about the durability of the bowling balls; they may be very fragile and shatter when dropped from the first floor, or they may be so tough that they shatter from a drop from the one-hundredth floor only.

This is a bowling ball stress test. What is the most efficient way to determine the floor from which a dropped bowling ball will shatter? In other words, what is the minimum number of bowling ball drops you need to guarantee you can identify the floor from which they will surely shatter? You are allowed to destroy both bowling balls in the tests, provided that in doing so you uniquely identify the correct floor.

Hint: Divide the job by skipping floors.

Candidates will want to clarify the problem. That's to be expected. This is a tricky problem, and candidates will want to know they are solving the right problem. The standard query is to make sure that if a bowling ball shatters from a drop from, say, floor 66, it will never shatter from a drop from floor 65. But most people get trapped by working the problem up a floor at a time. The flash of insight required is to realize that one can skip floors and, because there are two balls, work backward.

The solution either requires knowledge of number theory, experience with sampling for quality testing, or a bit of trial and error. Most interviewers stop the candidate as soon as they articulate an understanding of how to divide the 100 floors in the most efficient way or otherwise demonstrate the backtracking strategy. Listen to how one candidate restates the problem and then suggests a solution:

> The challenge here is to find the highest floor of a 100-story building from which the balls can be dropped without breaking, right? So the goal is to devise an optimal procedure that can always locate that floor using not more than n drop tests. What is the smallest n can be? We need a system. We can't use the obvious divide-by-2 search here because once the first ball breaks we'll need to search

all the untested floors below from bottom to top. To find the best strategy, I think we need to work backward from fewer floors using the following rule:

One drop allows us to test 1 floor.

Two drops can test 3 floors: Test the second floor first. If it breaks, test the first floor with the other ball. If not, test the top floor with either ball.

Three drops can test 6 floors: Test the third floor first. If it breaks, test the bottom 2 floors in order with the other ball. If not, test the top 3 floors as described above.

Four drops can test 10 floors: Test the fourth floor first. If it breaks, test the bottom 3 floors in order with the other ball. If not, test the top 6 floors as described above.

N drops allows you to test the number of floors equal to the sum of 1 to n. Fourteen drops can test 105 floors: Test the fourteenth floor first. If it breaks, test the bottom 13 floors in order with the other ball. If not, test the twenty-seventh floor next (14 + 13), and so on.

For any given drop, the number of drops you'll need after that should be the same if that ball breaks or not (or sometimes they are off by 1 if your total is not an even sum-of-1-to-n).

The optimum test protocol for 100 floors, then, requires a maximum of 14 drops. The next step is to derive a testing strategy that divides the 100 floors using the series 14 + 13 + 12 + 11 + 10 + 9 + 8 + 7 + 6 + 5 + 4 + 3 + 2 + 1. The best testing strategy starts with a drop from floor 14; then a drop from floor 27 (14 + 13); then 39 (14 + 13 + 12); etc. The full pattern is 14, 27, 39, 50, 60, 69, 77, 84, 90, 95, 99, 100.

In practice, this series sacrifices the first ball to point to an ever-decreasing series of possible target floors. A small number of drops using the second ball then identifies the target floor. Simply go back to the previously tested floor and start working up a floor at a time. Eventually, you will determine the floor at which the bowling ball shatters. This is the most efficient testing algorithm.

The absolute worst case is that the ball shatters on floor 13. Here's why. The first ball is shattered at floor 14. Then 13 more drops are required. Any other case requires fewer drops.

Let's assume the bowling balls shatter on, say, floor 73. You will drop the first ball six times (from floors 14, 27, 39, 50, 69, 77) and it shatters on the sixth test (floor 77). At this point, you have narrowed the target floor between floor 70 (you know the ball survived a drop from floor 69), and floor 77 (at which point it shattered). To test the specific floor from which a bowling ball shatters, simply increment from the last floor the ball survived and start testing according to the following protocol: 70, 71, 72, 73, at which point the second bowling ball will shatter and you will have your answer. For example, this test required 10 drops to identify the target floor.

If you get to floor 100 and the first ball hasn't shattered, you know you have a darn strong bowling ball. And it required only 12 drops to prove it.

Solution: Anywhere from 1 to 14 bowling bowl drops.

95 TWO WALKERS

The simplest puzzles continue to give candidates the most trouble. Most people have an intuitive reaction to the solution to this puzzle. It would be wrong. The following puzzle explores a very familiar theme but for some reason can be very perplexing.

Sally and John start off together on a one-mile walk to a nearby town. John walks at a constant speed. Sally's pace varies. For the first half mile, Sally walks at one mile per hour faster than John. For the second half mile, Sally walks one mile per hour slower than John. What happened as they reached the nearby town? Did they arrive at the same time, and if they didn't, who arrived first, Sally or John?

Hint: The math seems trivial. Work it out.

The obvious answer is that Sally and John would arrive at the same time because the effects of Sally's variable speed exactly cancel each other out. But in fact, no matter what Sally's speed is, John will always arrive first. This is one candidate's reasoning that a recruiter found very compelling:

> When Sally walks one-half of the distance one mile slower than John, she loses more than she gains when she walks the other half of the distance one mile per hour faster than John. For example, let's say that Sally's "fast" speed is three miles per hour, John's constant speed is two miles per hour, and Sally's "slow" speed is one mile per hour. Sally will cover the first half mile in 10 minutes and the second half mile in 30 minutes. However, John will cover the whole distance in only 30 minutes. This is because when Sally is traveling fast for half a mile, John is traveling two-thirds as fast as she is, but when Sally is traveling slow for half a mile, she's only traveling one-half as fast as John.

Solution: The constant-speed walker (John) will always beat the variable-speed walker (Sally).

96 HEADWIND, TAILWIND

This is a deceptive problem similar in design to the previous puzzle. Many recruiters select this puzzle when the candidate has arrived for the interview after taking a commercial airplane flight. Candidates are quick to get this puzzle wrong precisely because so many of us take airplane trips for granted and think we understand the additive concepts of speed. Recruiters look for candidates who really think the puzzle through and who reject the quick solution, even if they don't get the puzzle right at the end.

Consider a round-trip cross-country airplane flight, for example, from New York to Los Angeles and then back to New York. How will a constant and uniform wind affect the total elapsed time of the flights relative to no wind? Will a constant wind, uniform across both legs of the trip, make the total flight longer, make it shorter, or have no effect?

The obvious (and wrong) answer is to conclude that the effects of the headwind and tailwind will cancel each other out. In fact, wind will always add delay to the total flight. An understanding of the difference between an airplane's air speed and ground speed is useful. Consider the following scenario:

Suppose you have an airplane that flies 100 miles per hour relative to the ground. You need to make a round-trip flight between city A and city B (200 miles). The goal is to make the trip in the shortest possible time. Without a wind, the round-trip will take 4 hours. Now let's imagine a uniform wind speed of 50 miles per hour. The tailwind adds 50 miles per hour to the airplane's ground speed, resulting in the plane traveling at 150 miles per hour for the outbound leg of the round-trip. It will take 1 hour and 20 minutes for the first leg. The headwind subtracts 50 miles per hour from the speed of the airplane, resulting in a ground speed of 50 miles per hour. It will take 4 hours for the inbound leg of the round-trip. Going with the matching headwind and tailwind will cost us an extra hour and 20 minutes.

For a more rigorous proof of this somewhat startling result, consider this explanation:

Let s = plane's speed

w = wind speed

d = distance in one direction

Wind will add time to the flight by the ratio $(s^2)/(s^2 - w^2)$.

$d/(s + w)$ = time to complete leg flying with the wind

$d/(s - w)$ = time to complete leg flying against the wind

$d/(s + w) + d/(s - w)$ = round-trip time

$$\frac{d/(s + w) + d/(s - w)}{d/s + d/s}$$ = ratio of flying with wind to flying with no wind

This simplifies to $s^2/(s^2 - w^2)$.

The stronger the wind, the longer the trip will take, up until the wind speed equals the speed of the airplane, at which point the speed of the plane relative to the ground will be zero.

Solution: Any amount of wind will always make the round-trip flight longer.

97 PROGRAMMER'S DAUGHTERS

Here is another classic puzzle that tests a candidate's ability to listen for clues and manipulate numbers. Even people who have heard this problem before sometimes have trouble with it and need to rethink the whole thing.

Two senior programmers bump into each other after not having seen each other in 20 years.

"How have you been?" the first programmer says to the second.

"Great!" answers the second. "I have three daughters now."

"That's really great. How old are they?"

"Well, the product of their ages is 72, and the sum of their ages is the same as the number on that building over there."

"Right. I got it. Wait . . . I still don't know for sure."

"Oh, sorry," says the second programmer. "My oldest daughter just started to play the piano."

"Wonderful! My oldest is the same age!"

Problem: How old are the daughters?

Hint: Factors of success.

It's critical in puzzles like this to listen for all the clues and understand what information they communicate. The big insight is to know that the factors of 72 identify the ages of the daughters. You know this because 72 is the product of the ages of the three daughters. Most people actually list all the possible factors of 72.

Ages	Sum of ages
1 1 72	74
1 2 36	39
1 3 24	28
1 4 18	23
1 6 12	19
1 8 9	18
2 2 18	22
2 3 12	17
2 4 9	15
2 6 6	14
3 3 8	14
3 4 6	13

Why did the second man say he still did not know the daughters' ages? Because two sets of products add up to 14. So another clue is needed. In this case, the clue mentions that one of the girls is oldest. This clue eliminates one of the factors that feature two 6-year-old twins. The second set of factors that add up to 14 must be the ages of the daughters.

Why can we exclude the first three sets of factors? Because they would require the oldest daughter to be more than 20 years old, and the puzzle implies the daughters were born since the two men had last encountered each other, 20 years ago.

Solution: The daughters' ages are 3, 3, and 8.

Extra credit: One astute candidate pointed out that it is possible for two siblings to have the same age but not be twins; for instance one is born in January, and the next is conceived right away and delivered in October. Next October, both siblings will be one year old. The interviewer hired this candidate.

98 GUPPIES IN THE FISHBOWL

According to blogs of current and former Microsoft employees, this interview question has popped up on a fair number of interviews. NPR featured this puzzle on a program on Microsoft brainteasers. The announcer said that because the puzzle was still in use, the solution was "top secret." There's nothing secret about it, although like most good puzzles, the solution is surprising. The problem is simple from one perspective, but it can be distressingly difficult for candidates who don't take the mental shortcut.

There's a fishbowl with 200 fish, and 99 percent are guppies. How many guppies do you need to remove to get to the point where 98 percent of the remaining fish are guppies?

Hint: Don't get confused by the wording. You are not blindfolded. If you pick out a non-guppy, just throw it back. What needs to happen to get from 99 percent to 98 percent?

Just as important as the answer, the interviewer wants to hear how you got to the answer. So do your thinking out loud, and don't leave out any steps even if they are obvious. While it's possible to solve this problem with rigorous equations, it's better to think it out. Eve, a graduate student, introduces this solution, by blogging "I did oodles of these questions for my GRE when I applied for grad school, and I scored 100 percent on that section. I'm obsessed with puzzles":

The "top secret" solution is to realize that since you are taking out only guppies, the 1 percent of other fish you start with remains the same. One percent of 200 is 2 fish, so these 2 fish become 2 percent to make the guppies total up to 98 percent. Two fish of 2 percent is 100 total, so 100 guppies have to go.

A recruiter at Microsoft liked this candidate's take on the guppy problem:

Let's see . . . I'm only going to be removing guppies. That means the population of non-guppies remains the same. Okay, 99 percent of 200 fish means there are 198 guppies and 2 non-guppies. Now, how many guppies do I need so that, with 2 non-guppies, the guppies represent 98 percent of the bowl? The answer is 98. So I need to end up with 98 guppies from 198. That means I must remove 100 guppies.

Still not convinced? For mathematical support, I turned to Roger Breisch. His analysis:

Let x be the number of guppies to be removed. The total number of fish after removal is $200 - x$. The number of guppies after removal is $0.99 \cdot 200 - x$, or $198 - x$.

$$(198 - x)/(200 - x) = 0.98$$

$$198 - x = 0.98(200 - x)$$

$$198 - x = 196 - 0.98x$$

$$2 = 0.02x$$

$$x = 100$$

Solution: 100 guppies.

99 DIVIDING 17 HORSES AMONG THREE SONS

This is a classic puzzle that allows candidates to shine in two ways. The actual solution to the problem is one thing: it's elegant and satisfying. But explaining why the solution works is actually much harder and requires a deeper understanding of mathematics. Even candidates who know the solution have a hard time articulating the reason why it works, and interviewers always prefer the candidate who understands to the candidate who merely knows.

An aging father wants to divide his herd of 17 horses among his three sons. His will states that the oldest son gets half the herd, the middle son gets one-third of the herd, and the youngest son gets one-ninth of the herd. When the father dies, his sons are stumped about how to divide the herd because the desired fractions do not come out in whole numbers. As the sons argued, a traveling mathematician rode up on his horse, and upon hearing of the problem, he offered some advice that allowed the horses to be distributed to the three sons fairly and without harming any animals. What was the advice, how was the herd divided, and why does the solution work as it does?

Hint: What's the traveling mathematician traveling on?

It's possible to suggest creative metasolutions that do not really address the mathematical constraint. For example, my daughter Rachel, who is an equestrian, suggested that the traveling mathematician offer his horse as a sire to the mares of the herd, adding a sufficient number of foals to the herd to make the distribution trivial. But, rightly or wrongly, most interviewers are looking for a solution that explores the deeper mathematics of the puzzle.

So it's useful to review the math, just to have a baseline. There are 17 horses. By the father's terms, the oldest son gets half, or 8.5 horses; the middle son gets one-third, or 5.66 horses; and the youngest son gets one-ninth, or 1.88 horses. These fractions are not healthy for horses. So what the traveling mathematician can do is to add his own horse to the herd. Now there are 18 horses, and the sons can easily divide the herd.

The oldest son gets one-half, or 9 horses; the middle son gets one-third, or 6 horses, and the youngest son gets one-ninth, or 2 horses. Do the addition and you get 17 horses. The traveling mathematician reclaims his own horse and rides on, happy to be of service.

Solution: The traveling mathematician adds his horse to the herd, making 18 for easier division, and then take his horse back.

Extra credit: Pretty slick, right? But how does it work? The solution is fair, but only because everyone is happy. The problem is, the solution does not actually fulfill the terms of the will. The sons actually end up with more than their father intended to give them. By the precise terms of the will, the oldest son gets half, or 8.5 horses; the middle son gets one-third, or 5.66 horses; and the youngest son gets one-ninth, or 1.88 horses. But these don't add up to 17. There's about 0.875 horse left over. By the terms of the will nobody gets the remaining 0.875 horse. The traveling mathematician's clever solution is just a way of dividing up the remaining 0.875 horse among the three brothers so that all of them get whole horses, instead of fractions of horses. Another way to state the issue is to note that one-half (0.50) plus one-third (0.33333) plus one-ninth (0.11111) adds up to less than 1. The will did not say what to do with the extra 0.875 horse, so presumably it is fair to divide it among the sons.

100 FRACTIONAL VALUES

The eyes of most candidates completely glaze over as soon as they are presented with this puzzle. The first thing to do is relax. With a puzzle like this, there's always a trick or shortcut. No interviewer wants to stump you or watch you actually calculate this value. The interviewer wants to see how you react to a seemingly unmanageable puzzle. Do you panic and give up? Do you start working. Or do you start thinking?

What is the value of 1/2 of 2/3 of 3/4 of 4/5 of 5/6 of 6/7 of 7/8 of 8/9 of 9/10 of 1,000?

Hint: Work backwards.

This puzzle looks much more difficult than it is. The first thing is to look for a clue. That nice round final number of 1,000 is the place to start. Look for a series that reduces the value to another nice round number—either that or a zero along the way that reduces the eventual value to zero. But in this case, it's a series that actually solves for a nice round number. One good tactic for puzzles of this sort is to work backward. If you do, the problem becomes manageable. Working backward, 9/10 of 1,000 is 900; 8/9 of 900 is 800; 7/8 of 800 is 700; 6/7 of 700 is 600; 5/6 of 600 is 500; 4/5 of 500 is 400; 3/4 of 400 is 300; 2/3 of 300 is 200; and 1/2 of 200 is 100.

Solution: 100.

PROBABILITY PUZZLES

Many puzzles posed in job interviews feature probability-related themes. This should not be surprising. Many, perhaps most, business decisions have a critical element of probability at their core. Should we introduce a new product? What are the chances of its success? What is the likelihood our competitor will match us? What's the likelihood our medicine will win FDA approval? All these puzzles call on formal or informal understanding of such concepts as permutation, combination, sample spaces, and dependent and independent events. An understanding of these concepts and the ability to apply them to problems is an essential business skill.

101 BLINDFOLDED GRAB BAG

On one level, this is a simple arithmetic problem with a hint of probability tossed in. But the puzzle tests understanding of outcomes in an interesting way.

Assume you are blindfolded and placed in front of a large bowl containing currency in $50, $20, $10, and $5 denominations. You are allowed to reach in and remove bills, one bill at a time. The drawing stops as soon as you have selected four-of-a-kind— four bills of the same denomination. What is the maximum sum of money you could accumulate before the drawing ends?

Hint: Resist overconfidence. The interviewer expects you to think.

Many candidates guess, incorrectly, that the answer is $170—three $50 bills plus a $20 bill. But that misses the possibility that 12 bills could be drawn before picking four bills of the same denomination. The maximum value that can be picked is $305—three $50s, three $20s, three $10s, three $5s, and the last bill, that ends the selection, would be another $50 bill.

Solution: $305.

102 FUNNY COINS

This is a nice probability puzzle, not overly difficult but with a little edge. It requires the candidate to listen especially closely to the precise wording of the puzzle. As a general rule, it is always critical to listen to the precise wording of the challenge.

A gambler is holding three coins. One coin is an ordinary quarter, the second has two heads, the third has two tails. The gambler chooses one of the coins at random and flips it, showing heads. What is the likelihood that the other side is tails?

Hint: The challenge is not to calculate the probability of tails coming up.

Think this one through. How many heads and tails do these three coins represent? Three and three, respectively. It's tempting then, to conclude that there's a 50 percent chance of showing tails. But listen to the instructions. The gambler's first toss shows heads. The challenge is to calculate the probability that the other side of *this* coin shows tails. Since only one of the three coins has tails opposite, the answer is one out of three.

Solution: One-third.

103 DIALING FOR PHONE NUMBERS

Some recruiters like this puzzle because it involves a device and number sequences that are thoroughly familiar to most people. It is really a classic probability calculation.

If you were to randomly dial any seven digits on a telephone, what is the probability that you will dial your own seven-digit telephone number? Ignore area codes and assume we're in the United States.

Hint: Is every digit eligible for the first position?

Most interviewers just want to hear that the candidate understands two basic things. First, that the permutations for seven numbers are 10 raised to the seventh power. Second, that the conventions of telephone numbers actually reduce the number of available permutations. A recruiter especially appreciates this response:

> Let's assume that the first digit of the seven-digit number can be 2–9. We exclude 0 because it dials the operator and 1 because it indicates a long distance dialing code. The second to seventh digits of the number could be 0–9 Therefore the solution is:
>
> $$1/9 \cdot 1/10 \cdot 1/10 \cdot 1/10 \cdot 1/10 \cdot 1/10 \cdot 1/10 = 1/9,000,000$$
>
> If the first digit can be a zero, the answer would be 1 in 10,000,000.

Solution: 1 in 9,000,000.

104 MANHATTAN PHONE BOOK

There is a simple solution to this puzzle and a more sophisticated one. The smart candidate will answer one and then the other.

On the average, how many times would you have to flip open the Manhattan telephone book to find a specific name?

Hint: Listen to the wording of the problem. Answer the problem stated, not the one you think was intended.

The interviewer expects the candidate to address the probability question underlying the challenge, not to finesse the puzzle in some creative way, such as "I'd use the Internet white pages." So it would be useful to restate the problem: "By 'open,' I assume you are talking about opening the book to a random two-page spread. Should the desired name appear anywhere on the two exposed pages, the conditions would be satisfied." Assumptions are definitely allowed. Here's a response that one recruiter accepted:

> Let's assume the Manhattan telephone book has 1,000 pages. That means the book has 500 openings. The chance of flipping the book

open to any specific name is therefore 1 in 500. On the average, then, it takes about 500 flips to find a random name.

This analysis is technically correct, but it doesn't actually answer the question: *On the average, how many times would you have to flip open the Manhattan telephone book to find a specific name?* In other words, what's the average number of flips you would need to find the Manhattan listing for Bartholomew P. Wickershamer, Jr.? You could get lucky and find the listing on the first try. On the other hand, there are no guarantees. You could be flipping pages for years without landing on the right page.

The question asks for an average! So the recruiter really got excited with this next response, because the candidate not only had a better command of probability, but reframed the question in terms of confidence. The candidate further distinguished herself by displaying a key insight that business problems are often best represented not by a calculation of the probability of success, but by a calculation of the probability of failure.

Shouldn't the more precise question be, what is the chance of flipping to a wrong page? That's because we are going to keep flipping pages as long, and only as long, as we fail to find the right page. The real question is, how many times would we have to flip the book to achieve a given confidence level that at least one flip will be to the right page? The reality is that 100 percent confidence is impossible. We can never be 100 percent sure of flipping to the right page. So let's go for a more reasonable 50 percent confidence.

Given the 1,000-page telephone book, we know that the chance of flipping to the wrong opening on any given attempt is 499 out of 500, because all but one of the 500 possible openings are wrong. The chance that the first n flips will all fail to open to the right listing is then $(499/500)^2$. The chance that we'll flip open to the right opening in n flips or less is $1 - (499/500)^n$.

Most interviewers would be more than satisfied with this performance. But when the right candidate really gets into a puzzle, it is best to let him or her finish. This candidate opened a calculator to work out that the 50-50 odds of flipping to the correct page require 347 flips. The first answer of 500 flips actually gives a 63 percent confidence of finding the name. To achieve 90 percent confidence requires 1,150 flips.

105 PICK THE WHITE MARBLE AND WIN

This difficult puzzle is indicated for candidates for whom less challenging puzzles would be boring.

This is a game where you have white marbles and black marbles. If you pick a white marble, you win. If you pick a black marble, you lose. There are two jars, one with 50 white marbles, and one with 50 black marbles. Before you pick, you may distribute the marbles between the two jars in any way you wish. You must place all 100 marbles in the jars. Then the jars will be shaken up, and you will be blindfolded and presented with one of the jars at random from which you will draw 1 marble at random. How should you redistribute the marbles to maximize the probability that you pick a white marble and win?

Hint: Maximize chances in one bowl.

Here's how one candidate approached the puzzle. Notice how he used a collaborative style:

We have two choices to make. First we'll pick a jar, and each jar will have a 50 percent chance of being picked. Then we'll pick a marble, and depending how we distribute the marbles, we'll have a (# of white marbles in jar)/(# of total marbles in jar) chance of getting a white one. For example, say we put all the white marbles into jar A and all the black ones into jar B. Then our chances for picking a white one are:

50 percent chance we pick jar A · 50 percent chance we pick a white marble

50 percent chance we pick jar B · 0 percent chance we pick a white marble

That means we'll get a 100 percent chance for a white marble from jar A and a 0 percent chance for a white marble from jar B. The result? A 50 percent chance of picking a white marble. But we could have had the same result without putting all 50 white marbles in A. We could have put just 1 white marble in A and the odds would still be 1-1. So let's take all those other white marbles and throw them in jar B to help the odds out there. This way, we begin with a 50-50 chance of choosing the jar with just 1 white marble. And even if we choose jar B, we still have almost a 50-50 chance of picking 1 of the 49 white marbles.

Finally, let's do the math to calculate the optimum probability:

50 percent chance we pick jar A · 100 percent chance we pick a white marble

50 percent chance we pick jar B · 49/99 chance we pick a white marble

50 percent + 49/198 = 148/198 = 74.7474 percent.

With this optimum strategy, you can improve your chances of winning to almost 75 percent. Any other strategy will be inferior.

Solution: Place 1 white marble in jar A, and place the rest of the marbles (49 white, 50 black) in jar B.

106 MAXIMIZING THE ODDS
Programmers comfortable with algorithms tend to do well with this puzzle.

The candidate is presented with three index cards, face down. On each card, hidden from the candidate, is a random number. The objective is to choose the index card upon which is written the highest number.

Here are the rules: You can turn over any index card and look at the number written on it. If for any reason you think this is the highest number, you're done. Otherwise you discard that card and turn over a second index card. Again, if you think this is the one with the highest number, you may keep the second card, and the game is over. Or, you discard that one, too, and take your chance with the third card. Then the numbers on all three cards are exposed. If the card you have chosen has the highest number, you've won. If not, you've lost.

The challenge: The odds of selecting the highest number seem to be one in three. Or are they? Is there a strategy by which you can improve the odds?

Hint: Find a system by plotting out specific number combinations.

Chance predicts victory one-third of the time. But there is a better strategy to improve your odds. The following strategy changes the odds from one-in-three (33 percent) to one-in-two (50 percent). Here's how one candidate described the system:

> Take the first index card and discard it. Make a note of the number, but no matter how high it is, throw it away. Now pick the next card (it doesn't matter which). If the number on the second index card has a *higher* number than the first, retain the second index card. If the number on the second index card is *lower* than the first number, discard that one and select the third index card.
>
> By way of proof, consider the permutations. To really test this strategy, let's assume that the cards are marked A, B, and C. The first card, A, will always be discarded, so let's give it the highest value. Let's say the three index cards have numbers of 150, 25, and 50. Here's a chart that demonstrates the possible outcomes. The first column will always be discarded. Column 2 represents the second choice, and column 3 is the third card, which you may or may not get to. Here are the six possible outcomes:

A	B	C	Step	Outcome
150	25	50	Discard A, discard B, keep C	Lose
150	50	25	Discard A, discard B, keep C	Lose
25	50	150	Discard A, keep B, ignore C	Lose
50	150	25	Discard A, keep B, ignore C	Win
50	25	150	Discard A, discard B, keep C	Win
25	150	50	Discard A, keep B, ignore C	Win

Six possible combinations yield three wins and three losses: odds of one in two. Plug in any numbers. It doesn't matter.

Solution: Pick one card, note the number, and discard it. If the number on the second card is higher, keep it. If it's lower, discard it in favor of the third card.

107 IT'S A GIRL

A straightforward probability puzzle that has been around for years, yet continues to perplex.

You meet a stranger on the street, and ask how many children he has. He truthfully says two. You ask, "Is at least one of them a girl?" He truthfully says yes. What is the probability that the other one is a girl?

Before diving into a response, listen to the question. Repeat it once or twice. By now your ears should be alert to a peculiar phrase such as "at least." Ask yourself what that "at least" implies? If you don't, the obvious answer, of course, is 50-50. And, of course, the intuitive answer is wrong. Consider the four permutations:

Child 1	Child 2
1. Girl	Girl
2. Girl	Boy
3. Boy	Girl
4. Boy	Boy

The condition "at least one is a girl" eliminates only condition 4. There are three ways in which at least one of them could be a girl. And as a sibling of a girl in those three permutations, where there is girl, boy, or another boy, the chance of that sibling being a girl is only one out of three. A candidate explains:

The key is that we didn't specify which child was a girl, so it can be either one. If we had said instead, "The oldest child is a girl;

what is the chance that the other one is a girl?" the odds would be 50-50. But we just specified that "at least one" was a girl, so we don't know which it is and whether her sibling is a boy or a girl. And this means that the chances of that sibling being a girl are one out of three.

Solution: One-third.

108 CONVERSATION

This is a very difficult probability puzzle. It should be presented only to the most capable of candidates—and only if the interviewer has a deep understanding of the puzzle and its solution.

Imagine a job interview that consists of six interviewers sitting side by side along one side of a table, with you, the candidate, at one end. When I say "go!" everyone at the table begins a conversation with the person either to the left or to the right. Assuming that, on the command, people (except the ones at the ends, who have no choice) turn to either their right or their left at random, and assuming that those who find a partner at once in this way stick with that partner, and assuming that those who don't find a partner at once will behave rationally, doing their best to pair off with someone to their left or right, what is the probability that you will find yourself with no one to talk to?

Note the two conditions: (1) the randomness condition—at the word of command, the middle five people turn right or left at random—and (2) the rationality condition—that everyone thereafter behaves rationally. A recruiter who favors this puzzle considers this an ideal response:

There are seven people in a line. Call them A, B, C, D, E, F, and G. Let me be A, the candidate. The key to whether or not I get a conversation partner is of course the behavior of B. Since there are seven of us, one person is going to be left without a partner. B wants

131

to be sure it isn't him. In the absence of the randomness condition, B's best strategy would simply be to turn directly to me on the word "Go!" Since I, being at the end of the line, have no choices, he would then be certain to have a partner.

With the randomness condition imposed, things get trickier. On the word "Go!" each of the middle five people turns either left or right at random. There are 32 possibilities, which we could write out, if we wanted to, as

RRRRR

RRRRL

RRRLR

RRLRR

RLRRR

LRRRR

RLRRR

and so on

Sixteen of those possibilities begin with "L," that is, with B turned to the left, toward me. We strike up a conversation, and that's the end of that.

Of the remaining 16, there are 8 that begin with "RL" That is, B turned to his right, away from me, and C turned to his left, toward B. B and C struck up a conversation, I am out of luck, and that's that. The other 8 break out like this:

RRRRR

RRRRL

RRRLR

RRRLL

RRLRR

RRLRL

RRLLR

RRLLL

Consider the 2 that begin "RRRL," and look at them from the point of view of B (who is represented by that first "R"). C is facing away from him, but D and E have paired off. C has no choice but to turn to B. Neither, of course, have you. Thus B is certain to get a partner, no matter what he does!

So what does he do? What does "rational" mean in this circumstance? Well, it probably means something to do with the relative physical attractiveness of A and C, the odor of their breath, and other imponderables. From a game-theory—and also, I think from a commonsense point of view, B will turn either right or left at random again, since it makes no difference to him which he does. Since there are 2 possibilities out of 32 that this situation arose, there is a net 1 in 32 that he will turn to C.

In the other 6 cases

RRRRR

RRRRL

RRLRR

RRLRL

RRLLR

RRLLL

B's best move is to turn to me. My chance of being without a partner is therefore 8 out of 32 plus 1 out of 32, or 9/32.

Solution: The chance of the candidate being without a partner is 9/32.

109 SURVIVING LIARS AND TRUTH TELLERS

Here's a fun probability puzzle that uses the conventions of the Liars and Truth Tellers but in a novel way. It's based on a challenge that is found in many puzzle books and seems to delight programmers. The puzzle requires the candidate to dismiss many of the cases as irrelevant and to be able to focus on a limited number of outcomes. This ability is well suited to many businesses. This puzzle, originally called Killers and Pacifists, has been reworded because in this day and age talking of killers in an office environment makes many interviewers uncomfortable.

You enter a town that has L Liars and T Truth Tellers. When a Truth Teller meets a Truth Teller, nothing happens. When a Truth Teller meets a Liar, the Truth Teller disappears. When two Liars meet, both disappear. You may be a Truth Teller or a Liar. Assume meetings always occur between exactly two persons and the pairs involved are completely random. What are your odds of survival?

Hint: Eliminate irrelevant outcomes.

Regardless of whether you are a Truth Teller or a Liar, you may disregard all events in which a Truth Teller other than yourself is involved and consider only events in which you disappear or a pair of Liars other than yourself disappear. Thus we may assume that there are L Liars and yourself. If L is odd, your odds of surviving are zero. That's because as the Liars mutually annihilate, there will always be one left to make you disappear. If L is even, it doesn't matter to you whether you are a Liar or not. So assume you are. Then your probability of survival is $1/(L + 1)$.

Solution: $1/(L + 1)$.

110 SIMULTANEOUS BIRTHDAYS

When mathematicians gather in social settings, they often ask themselves questions like this. As a puzzle it can be entertaining because the solution is so surprising. Even candidates who have heard this puzzle will be challenged to explain the concepts underlying it.

How many candidates for a position does it take to know there's a 50-50 chance that 2 candidates share the same birthday?

The first thought is that it would take upwards of 150 people since there are 365 birth dates. But the solution is surprising. A college recruiter for Hewlett-Packard who uses this question found the following response ideal because it first simplified the challenge and then reframed it:

Let's first consider an applicant pool of only 2 candidates. What are the chances that they share a birthday? Although it seems like it's the same question, let's instead ask, what are the chances that they don't share a birthday? Since there are 365 days in the year, the second candidate can have any of 364 of them and not share a birthday with the first. Thus, the probability that they do not share birthdays is 364/365.

If a third candidate entered the room, what is the probability that none of them share birthdays? Well, the probability of the first and second candidates not sharing is 364/365. The probability of the third candidate not sharing a birthday with either of them is 363/365, given that the first and second have different birthdays. Thus the overall probability is (364/365)(363/365). A fourth candidate enters. Using the same logic, the probability of none of them sharing a birthday is (364/365)(363/365)(362/365). This can be represented as follows:

$$\frac{364}{365} \cdot \frac{363}{365} \cdot \frac{362}{365} = \frac{\frac{364!}{361!}}{365^3}$$

This statement can be generalized for an applicant pool including n candidates. The following equation uses this generalization in stating the original question—how many candidates does it take for the probability of at least 2 sharing birthdays to be greater than 1/2? (Remember that the probability of at least 2 candidates sharing a birthday is equal to 1 minus the probability that none share a birthday.)

$$1/2 < 1 - \frac{\frac{364!}{[364 - (n - 1)]!}}{365^{(n - 1)}}$$

Our goal is now to find the smallest n that satisfies this equation. The simplest way to accomplish this is a little trial-and-error. As it turns out, 23 is the magic number. When 23 candidates are convened together, there is a 50.7 percent chance that at least 2 will have the same birthday.

Solution: Twenty-three candidates have a 50-50 chance of sharing a birthday.

111 PLEASE TAKE YOUR SEATS AND FASTEN YOUR SEAT BELTS

This puzzle puts many people in the mind of the boarding process at Southwest Airlines, which stubbornly refuses to assign reserved seats.

A line of 100 airline passengers is waiting to board an airplane. They each hold a ticket to one of the 100 seats on that flight. For convenience, let's say that the nth passenger in line has a ticket for seat number n. Unfortunately, the first passenger in line ignores his or her assigned seat number and picks a random seat to occupy. All the other passengers are well behaved and will go to their assigned seats unless the seats are already occupied, in which case they also will take a seat at random. What is the probability that the last (one-hundredth) passenger to board the plane will sit in his or her assigned seat?

Hint: What happens on a plane with just two people?

Interviewers like this puzzle because it often flows naturally from conversation when the candidate flies in for the interview. A recruiter at Fog Creek Software recalls a candidate who answered:

This sounds like a recursive math problem, which, while not impossible, sounds like it's not what's called for here. So let's simplify and see if that helps. What if there were only two seats on the airplane? Then since he can sit in only one of two seats, he has a 50 percent chance of sitting in his assigned seat. Is this a general solution?

In the case of 100 seats on the airplane, can the last guy sit in, say, seat 75? No, because otherwise the seventy-fifth passenger would have sat in it. In fact, the one-hundredth guy can only be at seat 100 or 1. The one-hundredth guy doesn't decide anything. He takes whatever is available. So, don't mind him. So, there are only two possibilities, decided by guys 1 through 99. Since from everybody's point of view, seat 1 is just like seat 100 (they just look at their own seat as special and the first guy doesn't look at any seat as special), at the end, 1 being available must be just as likely as 100 being available.

For a formal proof, see http://discuss.fogcreek.com/techInterview/default.asp?cmd=show&ixPost=1710&ixReplies=8.

Solution: 50 percent chance.

PUZZLES FOR PROGRAMMERS AND CODERS

The puzzles in this chapter are the most difficult in the book. They should be used only for candidates who have demonstrated exceptional programming or puzzle-solving aptitude. For such candidates, these puzzles can discriminate between the stupendous and the merely out-standing. For anyone else, these puzzles will be very frustrating. In any event, any interviewer who intends to use these puzzles should have programming skills at least equal to that of the candidate.

These puzzles should not be used as a device to test specific coding skills. The best way to test the coding skills of programmers is to ask them to do structured coding. Rather than test coding skills per se, these puzzles provide interviewers with another set of data points to gauge to what extent a candidate "thinks" like a programmer, which is not at all the same thing as coding. There are lots of people who think like programmers and don't know Visual Basic from pig Latin. On the other hand, all these puzzles call on conventional programming experience and allow creative candidates to come to solutions much faster than candidates without such experience.

112 SNOOZE BUTTON

This puzzle finds favor in both software and hardware companies.

Many consumer alarm clocks have a snooze button that is calibrated for 9 minutes. Does that sound like an odd decision? Many people would think a 10-minute snooze interval would make more sense. So were the designers asleep? Why 9 minutes?

Hint: Minimize circuitry.

By setting the snooze time to 9 minutes, the alarm clock only needs to watch the last digit of the time. Whether implemented by physical circuitry or software, it is easier to manipulate just the terminal digit.

113 CHICKEN, FOX, AND GRAIN

This is perhaps the classic puzzle in this genre. Almost everyone knows it, so its use in a job interview may be suspect. Some interviewers ask candidates if they have ever heard it before and give points to those candidates who admit that they have. It is offered here to remind candidates of the "aha!" leap required to solve problems of this nature.

A farmer is standing on one bank of a river, with a fox, a chicken, and a bag of grain. He needs to get to the other side of the river, taking the fox, the chicken, and the grain with him. However, the boat used to cross the river is only large enough to carry the farmer and one of the things he needs to take with him, so he will need to make several trips in order to get everything across. In addition, he cannot leave the fox unattended with the chicken, or else the fox will eat the chicken; and he cannot leave the chicken unattended with the grain, or else the chicken will eat the grain. The fox is not particularly partial to grain and may be left alone with it. How can the farmer get everything across the river without anything being eaten?

Hint: Take something back across.

Many people struggle with this puzzle because of their one-way mode of thinking. It never occurs to them that they can take something back once they've transported it to the other side. An ability to solve this puzzle demonstrates a willingness to think outside the box and come up with creative solutions that still fit within the specified parameters.

Solution: The farmer takes the chicken across first, leaving the fox and grain together on the other side. He returns and gets the fox, but when he deposits the fox on the other side, he takes the chicken *back* across, so that the fox and chicken aren't left alone together. He drops the chicken off, picks up the grain, and takes it across to deposit with the fox. Finally, he returns to retrieve the chicken and takes it to the other side. At no time are the fox and chicken left alone together, nor are the chicken and grain.

114 100 PROGRAMMERS IN A ROW

This is a very difficult problem to solve during a job interview. Candidates need either a reasonable chunk of uninterrupted quiet time to address it or an interviewer willing to help guide them through the process. There are a number of approaches to this problem, with one being particularly elegant. Start with the obvious solutions and go deeper.

One hundred programmers are lined up one in front of the other by an evil human resources person such that programmers can see only the programmers in front of them. The HR person puts a red hat or a blue hat on every programmer. The programmers cannot see their own hats, nor can they see the hats of those behind them, but they can see the hats of the people in front of them. The HR person starts with the last programmer in the back and says, "What color is your hat?"

Programmers can answer with only one of two words, red *or* blue. *If the answer does not match the color of the hat on the person's head, the candidate is dismissed. Then the evil HR person moves on to the next programmer, going from the rear to the front of the row. Programmers in front get to hear the answers of the programmers behind them, but not whether they are dismissed or not. They can consult and agree on a strategy before being lined up, but after being lined up and having the hats put on, they can't communicate in any way other than by what has been specified.*

What strategy should the programmers select to guarantee the maximum number of surviving programmers?

Hint: Every programmer but the one challenged first can be saved.

Is the best strategy for every programmer to say the same color, let's say "red"? Assuming the hats were randomly distributed, half of them would survive. Another strategy calls for every programmer to identify the color of the hat on the head of the programmer immediately in front of him or her. This guarantees the survival of that programmer, but does nothing to promote the programmer's own chances for survival. This strategy also guarantees that at least half survive, plus a little more since chance predicts that some of the programmers would have hats of the same color as the person in front of them, thus sparing them both. In fact, assuming random distribution of hats, this strategy yields a survival rate of 75 percent. Getting better.

Some candidates might try to game the puzzle by suggesting that the people in the puzzle could agree to give clues to each other by using a certain tone of voice or drawing out the words. One candidate suggested that they could agree that if they said their hat color in a soft voice, it means the hat in front of them is the same color, and if they say it in a loud voice, it means the hat in front is a different color. Recruiters think this is definitely good and on the correct track. Another option is they could say "reeeeeeeeeeed" for x number of seconds, where x represented the distribution of hats where a hat was a bit in a binary number (red = 1, blue = 0).

But the ideal solution, according to most recruiters, acknowledges that the programmers can say only "red" or "blue" and cannot alter their voice in such a convincing way as to signal any information other than the word they said. A good way to get this point across is simply to change the problem slightly by saying "the evil HR person gets to hear their plan beforehand and will thwart it if it is not to the rules."

But even with the HR person hearing their plan in advance, there is still a way to save almost everyone. We know that the first programmer is never going to have any information about the color of his or her hat, so this person cannot be guaranteed to survive. But every other person can be saved with certainty. The programmers simply agree that if the number of red hats that the rear-most person can see is even, then the programmer will say "red." If the number of red hats that the rear-most person can see is odd, the programmer will say "blue." This way, programmer number 99 can look ahead and count the red hats. If the sum of red hats is an even number and number 100 said "red," then 99 must be wearing a blue hat. If they add up to an even number and number 100 said "blue," signaling an odd number of red hats, number 99 must also be wearing a red hat. Number 98 knows that 99 said the correct hat, and so uses that information along with the 97 hats in front to figure out what color hat is on the head of programmer 98.

Even if the evil HR person knows the plan, the person can't thwart it. The plan doesn't rely on any specific ordering of the hats. The worst outcome is that the evil HR person will ensure that programmer number 100 is dismissed.

115 DIGITAL KING

Programmers will probably delight in this puzzle. Everyone else will find it close to incomprehensible. A quintessentially binary problem, it goes to some programming techniques that most programmers use every day.

A ruthless king has a cellar of 1,000 bottles of very expensive wine. An assassin infiltrates the wine cellar to poison the wine. Fortunately the king's guards catch the plotter after she has

poisoned only one bottle. Unfortunately, the guards don't know which one of the bottles is poisoned. The poison is so strong that no amount of dilution will make it safe to drink. Furthermore, it takes one month to have an effect. The ruthless king decides he will get some of the prisoners in his vast dungeons to test the wine. Being an intelligent, if ruthless, king, he knows he needs to sacrifice fewer than 10 prisoners and know for a certainty which one of the wine bottles was poisoned. How does he know that?

Hint: If there were 1,024 or more bottles of wine, it would take more than 10 prisoners.

The solution to this puzzle should be familiar to any programmer:

Number the bottles 1 to 1,000, and write the number in binary format.

Bottle 1   = 0000000001

Bottle 250   = 0011111010

Bottle 1,000 = 1111101000

Now take prisoners 1 through 10 and let prisoner 1 take a sip from every bottle that has a 1 in its least significant bit. Let prisoner 2 take a sip from every bottle with a 1 in the next most significant digit. And so on until prisoner 10 takes a sip from every bottle with a 1 in its most significant bit. For example, take bottle 924:

Bottle 924   1 1 1 0 0 1 1 1 0 0

Prisoner   10 9 8 7 6 5 4 3 2 1

In other words, bottle 924 would be sipped by prisoners 10, 9, 8, 5, 4, and 3. That way if bottle 924 was the poisoned one, only those prisoners would die. After four weeks, the king lines the prisoners up in their bit order. In effect, the king reads each living prisoner as a 0 bit and each dead prisoner as a 1 bit. The number that the king derives from this strategy identifies the bottle of wine that was poisoned.

Extra credit: Mention that if the king really wanted to kill the least number of prisoners (and assuming he had a lot of prisoners at his disposal), the best strategy is to let 999 prisoners each take a sip from their respective bottle. That way, only the prisoner sampling from the poisoned bottle would die.

116 HANSEL AND GRETEL

A clever puzzle that tests the candidate's understanding of binary numbers.

Hansel and Gretel are taking a walk in the forest and want to find their way home. As they walk, they leave a repeating pattern of 1s and 0s behind them that they can follow home. What is the length of the shortest pattern such that if you happen along their trail, you can determine with certainty which direction they were going?

One solution is 010011, and it is probably the shortest. In a repeating series of this pattern, we may get . . . 110100110100110100110100110011 . . . . If we are to look through the sequence, we find that we can match the pattern 010011 but not the reverse pattern, 110010. Hence we know which direction the person was traveling.

Solution: 010011.

117 TWO TRAINS

Here's another challenge to write a program, except that the commands are specified.

A helicopter drops two trains, each attached to a parachute, onto a straight infinite railway line. There is an undefined distance between the two trains. Each faces the same direction, and upon landing, the parachute for each train falls to the ground next to the train and detaches. Each train has a microchip that controls its motion. The chips are identical. There is no way for the trains to know where they are. You need

to write the code in the chip to make the trains bump into each other. Each line of code takes a single clock cycle to execute. You can use the following commands (and only these):

MF—moves the train forward

MB—moves the train backward

IF (P)—conditional that's satisfied if the train is next to a parachute. There is no THEN to this IF statement

GOTO

One solution:

A: MF
IF (P)
   GOTO B
GOTO A

. . .

B: MF
GOTO B

The first line simply gets the trains off the parachutes. You need to get them off their parachutes so the back train can find the front train's parachute, creating a special condition that will allow it to break out of the code they both have to follow initially. They both loop through A: until the back train finds the front train's parachute, at which point it goes to B: and gets stuck in that loop. The front train still hasn't found a parachute, and so it keeps in the A loop. Because each line of code takes a "clock cycle" to execute, it takes longer to execute the A loop than the B loop. Therefore the back train (running in the B loop) will catch up to the front train.

118 PIRATE PUZZLE

This puzzle is reminiscent of the TV reality show Survivor, *in which contestants vote each other off an island in the hopes of being the sole winner of a cash prize. So this becomes a puzzle about taking risks, distributing profits, balancing competing interests, and building coalitions, all useful business skills. It is often included in interviews for programmers at New York–based Fog Creek Software. The pirate puzzle and its variations can be very intricate. Most candidates will need a few minutes of quiet time to tackle this puzzle. Interviewers are looking more for a specific insight than a full analysis of the puzzle.*

Five pirates have 100 gold coins. They have to divide up the loot. In order of seniority, each pirate proposes a distribution of the loot. All the pirates vote, and if at least half accept the proposal, the loot is divided as proposed. If not, the most senior pirate is eliminated, and they start over again with the next senior pirate. What solution does the most senior pirate propose? Assume they are very intelligent, extremely greedy, and interested in surviving.

Hint: Who said anything about fairness?

Puzzles of this type require the candidate to enter an abstract world populated by perfectly logical beings. It's best to forget most of what you know about how people really act. The people in puzzles operate in a rarefied atmosphere and are concerned only with getting the best outcome for themselves. They make immediate decisions—randomly, if necessary. They draw precise conclusions about the predictable behavior of other players in the puzzle.

A recruiter who has given the pirate puzzle many times says: "Many candidates quickly suggest something like, 'The most senior pirate takes half and divides the rest up among the least senior pirates.' No, that misses the whole point. Any response without a specific strategy behind it is invalid. If I ask you why a senior pirate would give anything to a junior pirate, I don't want to hear 'because he's fair.' There's nothing about fairness in the statement. I want to hear the leap that solves the problem. Once I hear it, I usually don't take the time for candidates to finish the puzzle."

The key insight is that the senior pirate needs to get the cooperation of the junior pirates (the same thing is required for the success of a development project). In other words, what's to stop the rest of the pirates from voting in a bloc against your plan and eliminating you? Then there would be only four pirates to share 100 coins, not five.

The base situation is one pirate. Obviously he would keep all 100 coins for himself. How about two pirates? The following candidate nailed the puzzle by saying:

> The most senior pirate knows that he needs to get two other pirates to vote for his solution in order for him not to be eliminated. So why would any pirate vote for him? The next most senior pirate would surely see it in his self-interest for the senior pirate to be eliminated. Let's start simplifying. If there were only one pirate, there would be no puzzle. The pirate would take all the loot, and no one would complain.
>
> Now consider the situation with two pirates. Same outcome. The senior pirate takes all the loot, and the other pirate can't do a thing about it as the senior pirate's vote represents half of the voters.
>
> It gets more complicated for the senior pirate when there are three pirates. Let's number the pirates from least to most senior: 1, 2, and 3. With three pirates, pirate 3 has to convince at least one other pirate to join his collation. Pirate 3 realizes that if his plan is not adopted, he will be eliminated, and they will be left with two pirates. All of them know what happens when there are two pirates: pirate 2 takes all the loot himself and pirate 1 gets nothing. So pirate 3 proposes that he will take 99 gold coins and give 1 coin to pirate 1. If pirate 1 has any self-interest at all, he really has no choice. If pirate 1 rejects the offer, he gets nothing. So pirate 3's plan will pass two to one over pirate 2's objection.
>
> With four pirates, an even number, the senior pirate needs just one vote other than his own to impose his will. His question now is which one of the other pirates' votes can be exchanged for the fewest number of coins. Pirate 2 recognizes that he is most vulnerable. Therefore, pirate 4 knows that if he gives pirate 2 anything at all, he will vote for it.
>
> A rule is emerging here. In each case, the senor pirate should buy only the votes he needs, and buy them as cheaply as possible. Apply the rule to the five-pirate case. Pirate 5 needs two votes plus his own. The goal is to toss a coin or two to pirate 1 and pirate 3, the two pirates in the most vulnerable positions. Both will be empty-handed

if the senior pirate is eliminated and four pirates remain. So pirate 5 offers one coin to pirate 3 and one coin to pirate 1. Pirates 2 and 4 get nothing.

For a fuller discussion of this puzzle solution, check out Fog Creek Software programmer Michael Prior's solution at http://techinterview.org/Solutions/fog0000000102.html.

Solution: The pirate offers one coin each to the pirates in the first and third positions.

119 COUNT IN BASE −2

At first glance this puzzle makes no sense. The fact is, there is no base −2. Nevertheless this puzzle is occasionally used at Microsoft job interviews to test programmers who have passed every other test.

Count in base −2.

Hint: Think about binary notation and extrapolate.

Ole Eichorn, who runs a blog called *The Critical Connection* (http://w-uh.com/) and hires programmers using this puzzle, likes the information it gives him. He takes a crack at the puzzle like this:

This question is a little troublesome in that if the candidates have encountered it before, they'll probably breeze through it, and if they haven't, it might take them a moment to get their mind around the concept of a "negative base." So, a negative base. What does "base" really mean? Well, it determines the base for an equation of the form:

$$c_n b^n + c_{n-1} b^{n-1} + \ldots + c_1 b^1 + c_0 b^0$$

The c coefficients are the digits in a number. If $b < 0$, then the factors with even exponents will be positive, but the factors with odd exponents will be negative. This makes for some slight weirdness. A system with base −2 needs two-digit values; let's call them 0 and 1. Then:

$$1 = 1$$
$$10 = -2$$

$$100 = 4$$
$$1000 = -8$$
$$10000 = 16$$

And so on. Counting is a little counterintuitive. Here are the first few integers:

$$1 = 1$$
$$2 = 110 \ (4 + -2!)$$
$$3 = 111$$
$$4 = 100$$
$$5 = 101$$
$$6 = 11010 \ (16 + -8 + -2, \text{if you get this, you've got them all})$$
$$7 = 11011$$
$$8 = 11000$$
$$9 = 11001$$

If candidates get this far, I'd give them full credit. However, for extra credit they might note that this binary sequence also contains negative numbers! Here are the first few negative integers:

$$-1 = 11 \ (-2 + 1)$$
$$-2 = 10$$
$$-3 = 1101 \ (-8 + 4 + 1)$$
$$-4 = 100$$
$$-5 = 1111 \ (-8 + 4 + -2 + 1)$$
$$-6 = 1110$$
$$-7 = 1001$$
$$-8 = 1000$$

This is a pretty cool thing—that by using a negative base, all the integers are representable in binary! If a candidate thought this was cool, too, I'd think the candidate was cool, too.

In his book *How Would You Move Mount Fuji* (see Appendix E), William Poundstone develops a notation using base −2 and comes up with the following values for the first 10 numbers:

1	1
2	110
3	111
4	100
5	101
6	11010
7	11011
8	11000
9	11001
10	11110

BUSINESS CASES

Job interviews at consulting firms typically feature a specific type of mental challenge called case interviews or business cases. Business cases are word problems based on real-life or hypothetical business situations. Today, financial, marketing, and operations environments are also using business cases to screen candidates on the ability to think quickly and logically about business problems, to demonstrate analytical skills, and to showcase interpersonal skills. Business cases come in a variety of flavors.

COMPREHENSIVE CASES

These are elaborate business strategy or operations scenarios that can take the candidate up to an hour to analyze. Most MBA graduates will be familiar with these types of cases. The content of the case will depend on the functional area in which the candidate is interviewing, and may call on marketing, operations, strategic, and financial skills. An example of a consulting case question might be: "Should the company develop needed technology, or buy it by licensing the technology or acquiring a company?" This case may be a monologue, in which candidates analyze the case without dialogue, or may be interactive, in which candidates are encouraged to interrogate the interviewer. Comprehensive cases tend to be deductive or inductive.

Deductive Cases

These cases argue from the general to the specific and have these attributes:

- Provide you with very little information
- Test your ability to probe for additional details
- Require structuring framework based on new facts

Inductive Cases

These cases argue from the specific to the general and have these attributes:

- Provide you with a significant amount of detail, some unnecessary
- Test your ability to distill key issues
- Require depth of analysis based on relevant facts

GROSS ORDER OF ESTIMATION CASES

Also known as market-sizing problems or Fermi questions (see Chapter 9), these challenges are designed to gauge how comfortable candidates are with numbers and whether they can quickly zero in on market drivers, make reasonable assumptions, and work through to a defensible guesstimate. Usually, the interviewer neither knows the answer to the question nor cares about it.

Accenture, a global management consulting firm with offices in 48 countries, avoids the use of brainteasers, but does present cases at job interviews. Accenture interviewers look for a reasoned, systematic approach to each case rather than for a specific answer. "There are usually several credible approaches and solutions; it is most important to provide a thoughtful, structured response. You are not expected to have deep industry knowledge related to the case—but you are expected to be effective with the knowledge you do have and make hypotheses based on sound common sense," notes an Accenture recruiter. To help candidates with the case interview, Accenture, like most other consulting firms, has a Web page to guide candidates through a structured approach to problem solving.

SUGGESTED METHODOLOGY

Approaching a business case requires a disciplined methodology. The answer is always less important than the methodology you select. Different firms and different interviewers have different case styles. Be sensitive to the hints, data, or suggestions of the interviewer. Usually, the interviewer wants to hear you think out loud and to hear what approaches you are considering and rejecting. If you get stuck, the interviewer will usually guide you in the direction he or she wants you to go. The business case interview frequently involves market analysis or new-product development. There are several questions you can ask and steps you can take to ensure that you have covered most of the main points. In addressing business cases involving gross order of estimation, keep these six points in mind:

1. *Identify the problem.* The interviewer will begin by verbally outlining a case situation (e.g., profits are declining in the men's wear division). Listen carefully and request permission to take notes. Write down the recruiter's main points. Ask, identify, and confirm the following: What are the company's short-term and long-term objectives—what is it trying to accomplish? Although the company's objectives may seem obvious, do not assume them. There are often hidden agendas in objectives. It is always a good policy and good business to ask. You can be sure that consultants always ask their clients.

2. *Back translate.* That is, repeat what you have just heard. You do this for several reasons: First, you get to hear the case all over again. Second, you show the interviewer that you were listening. And third, you do not end up answering the wrong question, which happens more often than you think and is grounds for dismissal if this occurred on a job.

3. *Develop a hypothesis.* Many firms follow a hypothesis-based approach, which calls for the interviewee to develop a hypothesis early on regarding the nature of the business issue. While some firms prefer this up-front hypothesis, others prefer you skip this step and work toward a hypothesis and recommendation at the conclusion of the case.

   As you gather data in the time that follows, you are working to prove this hypothesis. If you gather enough data to refute your hypothesis, you should redefine your hypothesis and proceed. A diagram of the situation may help you think clearly as you dissect the issues.

4. *Establish a "framework" or a series of frameworks to structure your analysis.* A framework is a structure that you use to organize your

thoughts and help you analyze the critical issues of a case, such as the cost-benefit model or Porter's five forces. Choosing a framework is not the main goal of this exercise—it is meant only to guide you. Allow your own creativity to come through rather than being overly reliant on the framework. If a single framework could solve the problem, the interviewer probably would have presented a different case.

After you have decided how you are going to structure your analysis, communicate this so that the interviewer understands the way in which you are approaching the problem.

5. *Gather data and test your hypothesis.* Begin by asking the most basic questions. Work your way methodically through, starting with the most important issue. Your framework will guide you in covering your major points for in-depth analysis in the time allowed. Remember that the case facts may be intentionally ambiguous—keep probing to get the information you need. Don't forget to delve into the industry, competitors, overall corporate strategy, effects on suppliers and buyers, and other internal and external factors.

Think out loud! Let the interviewer see how you are analyzing the problem by voicing your thought process and assumptions.

6. *Identify alternatives*

- Discuss the costs and benefits of each alternative, including your reasons for discounting their relevance in the particular situation. Clearly state your assumptions and your rationale.

- Conduct a sensitivity analysis to determine how sensitive the results are to any assumptions you may have made.

- Make a recommendation.

- Summarize your analysis and the approach you used.

- Summarize your main findings, stating the main supporting facts you have gathered and the relevant assumptions you have made.

- Make a solid, data-driven recommendation, choosing an alternative that has a positive net present value and is consistent with the strategy of the firm.

- Indicate the next steps and additional analysis needed (do not recommend additional analysis be done before a recommendation can be given—a solid recommendation should always be given, followed by a statement of steps you would take prior to implementing that recommendation, if necessary).

- After your recommendation, an assessment of the risks of your recommendation is an added plus ("The risks of this solution are . . . ").

The whole purpose of a case interview is for the recruiter to test your ability to dissect a problem in a logical fashion. Therefore, in your analysis, make sure to justify all your assumptions and decisions. When faced with a complex problem, break it down into manageable portions, and develop a decision tree to arrive at your solution. Doing this will allow you to retrace your thought process and proceed down a different path if your first solution is not optimal.

Do not be afraid to ask questions when you need more information; the opening dialogue may be intentionally vague. You are not expected to know everything, but your ability to ask pointed, probing questions will shed light into your logical thought process.

120 ACCENTURE BIOTECHNOLOGY CASE

This case study used by Accenture (www.accenture.com) outlines a situation and provides you with some of the key issues and potential questions you may want to consider. Spend some time thinking about the situation and working through the structured problem-solving process as you would in an interview.

The client is a U.S. biotechnology company with one product on the market ($500 million in sales). The task, or business problem, is to help the client think through the question, "Should we invest money in expanding our sales force?"

Some facts:

- Product is used by dialysis patients; target audience is nephrologists.
- In 6 to 12 months, company is planning on introducing a new product to the market.

CHAPTER 8

- New product is for cancer patients; target audience will be oncologists.

- There is one major competitor for current product; if new product is introduced within a year, there will be no competition for at least one year.

- Current sales force consists of 100 sales representatives.

- Most reps joined company to be in an entrepreneurial environment.

- Company has been selling only one product for the past five years.

- To successfully introduce new product to the oncology market, company will need to invest money in expanding its sales force.

Additional industry background:

- The life of a patent is 17 years; however, most of this life is spent in the R&D and FDA approval processes.

- Being first to market is extremely important to a new product's success.

- Selling cycle: Sales reps call on doctors to discuss products → Doctors recommend products to patients → Patients choose and buy products to use → Health plan or insurance company reimburses patients.

- Cancer products are generally very expensive; however, most of the patient's out-of-pocket costs are covered by the patient's health plan or insurance company.

- To sell cancer products to oncologists requires experienced salespeople with technical backgrounds (oncologists do not see sales reps easily) — it usually takes 6 to 12 months to recruit and train a new sales team.

Key Issues—Problem Decomposition

The interviewer may ask the candidate to consider any of the following probing questions. The expectation is that the candidate will base answers on the evidence.

- What is the potential demand (in units) for the new product?

- How many cancer patients are there?

- How often will patients use the product?

- What is the recommended dosage per usage occasion?
- What unit price will the company be able to charge for the new product?
- How will price be set for the product in the marketplace?
- What is the size of the sales force investment that will be required to support the new product?
- What is the average annual cost of a sales rep?
- How many additional sales reps will be needed to successfully introduce and adequately support the new product?
- How many oncologists will need to be called upon?
- How often will each oncologist need to be called?
- What will be the average length of an oncologist call?
- Where is the point of diminishing returns for sales calls?
- How will potential demand be impacted by the number of sales reps selling the new product?
- How would you estimate demand for the new product?
- What approach would you use and what data would you want to see?
- How would you set the price for the new product?
- Is this product likely to be price elastic or price inelastic?
- What if there was competition for the new product?
- If the client decided to invest, should the client go with one combined sales force (for both products) or two separate sales forces (one for each product)?
- What factors would you want to consider in deciding between one or two sales forces?
- How similar are the two products and target audiences?
- Are the two target audiences located in geographic proximity to each other?
- Will the new product distract sales reps from selling the current product (or vice versa)?

121 CAPITAL ONE TELEPHONE CARD CASE

Capital One (www.capitalone.com) is the leading credit card issuer. It has a customer base of 47 million and managed loans of over $70 billion. The company's employee selection process generally includes case interviews for many management and information technology candidates, with the mathematical complexity of the case varying depending on the specific position. In addition, all on-campus recruiting interviewees should expect to encounter a case interview.

You have just been appointed the manager of the cross-sells team at Capital One, which evaluates opportunities to market non–credit card products to our credit card customers. These cross sells usually involve building relationships with outside vendors who sell us products that we, in turn, can sell to our customers at a premium.

One potential cross-sell opportunity that is sitting on your desk right now is the prepaid phone card—a piece of plastic you can use to pay for long distance telephone calls. You use the card by calling a 1-800 number, entering the card's PIN number, and then entering the destination telephone number. The minutes left on the card are tracked by the outside vendor—your only responsibility is to market the product in a way that maximizes profit for Capital One.

Probing question: What are the salient questions you need answers to at this point?

The case outlines a situation and provides you with some of the key issues and potential questions you may want to consider. Capital One case interviews are dynamic, one-on-one interactions with an interviewer. Candidates are encouraged to ask intelligent questions and engage in discussion around the problem. Capital One's case interviews feature a highly quantitative focus because they are representative of the problems that Capital One managers face.

Often, the interviewer prefaces the case with these words: "This interview will give you an opportunity to exercise your conceptual, quantitative, and analytical reasoning skills, and usually includes the use of mathematics to arrive at the best solution. But solid quantitative skills aren't the only thing we're looking for—we're also interested in your leadership experience, communication skills, creativity, and flexibility."

Below is a list of some of the most important questions you should have.

- How much does each phone card cost Capital One?

- Are there any other costs involved, such as a setup fee?

- Are there any constraints on how many minutes each phone card has?

- Are there any constraints on how much the cards can sell for?

- How much do competitors charge for their phone cards?

- How much do Capital One's cross-sell products usually sell for?

- How many customers usually buy Capital One's cross-sell products?

- What distribution channels are available for marketing the phone cards to customers?

- How much would this marketing cost?

The interviewer continues: "Luckily, the vendor who wants to sell us the phone cards has already sent an introductory e-mail that provides a lot of the information you need. The e-mail has several key points:

- The card may be sold at any price. Other companies have sold the cards for up to $0.75 per minute.

- The card may be sold with any number of minutes on it.

- Capital One must pay $0.20 per minute sold.

- Capital One must pay $2 per card sold for account set-up, which includes card materials, the vendor's system programming, and postage.

- The vendor notes that the phone card could be a good addition to Capital One's cross-sell program, which ordinarily offers products in the $5 to $30 price range.

"Let's assume that Capital One has decided to sell 60-minute phone cards at a price of $30 each. How much profit do we make on each card sold?"

First Answer

Capital One's profit per card is $16. The equation is shown below.

$$X = \text{Profit per card sold}$$

$$X = (\text{Revenue per card}) - (\text{expense per card})$$

$$X = \$30 - [(\$0.20 \cdot 60) + \$2.00]$$

$$X = \$16$$

Probing question: Is this equation complete? Is there anything big missing from this picture?

The thing that we haven't considered yet is marketing costs. (In reality, we haven't considered several things, but the lack of marketing expense has the biggest impact by far.) Basically, it will cost Capital One some money to tell our customers about the phone card offer, but we didn't include any of that expense in the preceding equation.

But how should we market this product? There are several different distribution channels we could use.

- *Statement inserts.* Little slips of paper we put inside customers' monthly statements, which they return to us when they mail us their payments.
- *Statement messages.* A line or two of text typed on the remittance stub of each statement (the part a customer rips off and mails back with the check). It might say something like, "Check this box if you would like to purchase a Capital One phone card, good for 60 minutes of long distance calling, for only $30!"
- *Bangtails.* Slips of paper that are attached to the backs of the envelopes that customers use to mail in their payments. If the cusomers are

interested in the product, they can rip off the stubs and put them inside the envelopes.

- *Direct mail.* We could send our customers a letter—separate from their monthly statement—describing the phone cards in detail.

- *Outbound telemarketing.* We could place telephone calls to our customers describing the cards and asking them if they would like to purchase one.

Please take a few moments to think about the distribution channels above. How are they similar? How are they different?

What factors would be most important in determining which distribution channel you should use? In other words, what additional information would you need to know about each channel to decide which is best? For the purposes of this case, you do not need to think about all the variables for every distribution channel—just try to think of the two main variables that apply to all of them.

The two most important factors you need to consider are cost and response rate.

- *Cost.* It is easy to see that cost will vary a lot depending on what distribution channel we decide to use. For example, with outbound telemarketing, we have to pay the salary of the telemarketer plus the cost of the call (or outsource the job to a professional telemarketing firm, which isn't cheap, either). If we decide to use direct mail, we will need to pay the cost of printing the letter and other marketing materials, plus the envelope, plus the postage. On the other extreme, if we decide to go with statement questions, then it costs us nothing—we already print statements anyway, and we have automated scanners to capture the responses.

- *Response rate.* The percentage of customers we solicit who decide to purchase the phone card will vary considerably as well. And as we might suspect, cost and response rate are often positively correlated—the more a marketing effort costs, the more people respond to it, and vice versa. For example, a lot of people might respond to a direct-mail solicitation, but far fewer would respond to the statement question. After all, it's hard to miss a letter in your mailbox, but customers could easily overlook a line or two at the bottom of their statement. Plus if we send out a letter, we have a lot of room to include persuasive text and beautiful photos discussing the benefits of the phone card, but if we decide to go with a statement question, we have only two short lines of text to make the sale. Having more space and flexibility to promote the product would have a big impact on what percentage of people choose to buy it.

There are lots of other factors you might have thought of that also deserve consideration. A few are outlined briefly below:

- *Time to market.* It takes a lot more time to use some of these channels than others. If we thought other companies were going to increase their marketing of phone cards in the near future, we might decide to use a channel that gets us to market fastest.

- *Operational impact.* To get things going, one channel might take a few hours of a single person's time, whereas another channel might require us to mobilize an entire department for a week. Although this sort of implication can be included in the "cost" consideration above, it is also valuable to consider it separately.

- *Customer perception and preference.* Some customers don't like receiving telemarketing calls, so we need to consider this when formulating our marketing campaigns.

Probing question: Assuming 60-minute cards must sell for $30, what response rate would be required to break even on the insert?

Hint: Breaking even *means that you neither gain money nor lose money on a project—your total profit is $0. The breakeven point for a given variable is a very useful figure in business since it tells you the point when you start making (or losing!) money.*

There are a number of different ways you could have chosen to solve this problem, but the answer is the same no matter which way you do it.

Method 1

Assume that you mail 100 inserts, and then determine how many people would have to respond for the profit to equal zero.

$$\text{Let } R = \text{the number of responders}$$

$$(\text{Revenue per card sold}) - (\text{expense per card sold}) = 0$$

$$\$30R - [(\$0.20 \cdot 60)R + \$2.00R + (100 \cdot \$0.04)] = 0$$

$$30R - 12R - 2R - 4 = 0$$

$$16R = 4$$

$$R = 0.25 \text{ people per hundred}$$

$$R = 0.25 \text{ percent}$$

Method 2

Same as method 1, except you don't assume a certain number of customers.

$$\text{Let } R = \text{response rate}$$

$$(\text{Revenue per card sold}) - (\text{expense per card sold}) = 0$$

$$\$30 - [(\$0.20 \cdot 60) + \$2 + (\$0.04/R)] = 0$$

$$30 - 12 - 2 - (0.04/R) = 0$$

$$(0.04/R) = 16$$

$$16R = 0.04$$

$$R = 0.25 \text{ percent}$$

Method 3

Breakeven occurs when (profit per piece mailed) − (marketing cost per piece mailed) = 0

$$\text{Response rate } R = (\text{\# of cards sold/\# of pieces mailed})$$

You can multiply any expression by $(1/R) \cdot R$, or (# pieces mailed/# cards sold) · (# cards sold/# pieces mailed), since this expression is equal to 1.

Recall from the assumptions that marketing cost per piece mailed = $0.04.

$$(\text{Profit/piece mailed}) \cdot (\text{\# pieces mailed/\# cards sold})$$
$$\cdot (\text{\# cards sold/\# pieces mailed}) - \$0.04 = 0$$

After you cancel out "pieces mailed" from the first two elements of the equation above, you get the following equation:

$$(Profit/card\ sold) \cdot (\#\ cards\ sold/\#\ pieces\ mailed) - \$0.04 = 0$$

This evaluates to

$$(Profit/card\ sold) \cdot R - \$0.04 = 0,$$

since $R = (\#\ cards\ sold/\#\ pieces\ mailed)$.

Recall from earlier in the case that the profit per card (without marketing expense) is $16. Therefore

$$\$16R - \$0.04 = 0$$

$$R = 0.25\ percent$$

Any way you look at it, the answer is the same—if more than 0.25 percent of customers who receive the phone card offer decide to purchase a card, then Captial One will make a profit. If fewer than 0.25 percent of customers respond, then Captial One will lose money.

Does 0.25 percent sound like a reasonable expectation? Although it's impossible to tell in advance what the actual response rate would be, 0.25 percent sounds achievable, and so the phone card cross sell is definitely worth testing.

122 BOSTON CONSULTING GROUP RETAILING CASE

Boston Consulting Group (BCG) expects candidates to be able to digest a great deal of information, understand the objective of the hypothetical consulting engagement, and then speak intelligently about a process that will yield a solution. This business case, once outlined on BCG's Web site, is particularly valuable because it takes the candidate through a typical exchange between the interviewer and the candidate. And while the framework it outlines is valuable, even more compelling is the quality of the conversation.

Your client is the largest discount retailer in Canada, with 500 stores spread throughout the country. Let's call it CanadaCo. For several years running, CanadaCo has surpassed the second

largest Canadian retailer (300 stores) in both relative market share and profitability. However, the largest discount retailer in the United States, USCo, has just bought out CanadaCo's competition and is planning to convert all 300 stores to USCo stores. The CEO of CanadaCo is quite perturbed by this turn of events and asks you the following questions: "Should I be worried? How should I react?" How would you advise the CEO?

Hint: Note the three questions to be answered.

The first step, as always, is to establish an understanding of the case. Asking questions is a good way to start, although to my mind the first question is too elementary:

> CANDIDATE: So, the client, CanadaCo, is facing competition in Canada from a U.S. competitor. Our task is to evaluate the extent of the threat and advise the client on a strategy. Before I can advise the CEO, I need some more information about the situation. First of all, I'm not sure I understand what a discount retailer is.

> INTERVIEWER: A discount retailer sells a large variety of consumer goods at discounted prices, generally carrying everything from housewares and appliances to clothing. Kmart, Woolworth, and Wal-Mart are prime examples in the United States.

The candidate is then expected to set up the framework for engaging the case:

> CANDIDATE: Oh, I see. Then I think it makes sense to structure the problem this way: First, let's understand the competition in the Canadian market and how CanadaCo has become the market leader. Then let's look at the United States to understand how USCo has achieved its position. At the end, we can merge the two discussions to understand whether USCo's strength in the United States is transferable to the Canadian market.

> INTERVIEWER: That sounds fine. Let's start, then, with the Canadian discount retail market. What would you like to know?

> CANDIDATE: Are CanadaCo's 500 stores close to the competition's 300 stores, or do they serve different geographic areas?

INTERVIEWER: The stores are located in similar geographic regions. In fact, you might even see a CanadaCo store on one corner and the competition on the very next corner.

CANDIDATE: Do CanadaCo and the competition sell a similar product mix?

INTERVIEWER: Yes. CanadaCo's stores tend to have a wider variety of brand names, but by and large, the product mix is similar.

CANDIDATE: Are CanadaCo's prices significantly lower than the competition's?

INTERVIEWER: No. For certain items, CanadaCo is less expensive, and for others the competition is less expensive, but the average price level is similar.

CANDIDATE: Is CanadaCo more profitable just because it has more stores, or does it have higher profits per store?

INTERVIEWER: It actually has higher profits than the competition on a per-store basis.

CANDIDATE: Well, higher profits could be the result of lower costs or higher revenues. Are the higher per-store profits due to lower costs than the competition's or the result of higher per-store sales?

INTERVIEWER: CanadaCo's cost structure isn't any lower than the competition's. Its higher per-store profits are due to higher per-store sales.

CANDIDATE: Is that because it has bigger stores?

INTERVIEWER: No. CanadaCo's average store size is approximately the same as that of the competition.

CANDIDATE: If they're selling similar products at similar prices in similarly sized stores in similar locations, why are CanadaCo's per-store sales higher than the competition's?

INTERVIEWER: It's your job to figure that out!

CANDIDATE: Is CanadaCo better managed than the competition?

INTERVIEWER: I don't know that CanadaCo as a company is necessarily better managed, but I can tell you that its management model for individual stores is significantly different.

CANDIDATE: How so?

INTERVIEWER: The competitor's stores are centrally owned by the company, while CanadaCo uses a franchise model in which each individual store is owned and managed by a franchisee who has invested in the store and retains part of the profit.

CANDIDATE: In that case, I would guess that the CanadaCo stores are probably better managed, since the individual storeowners have a greater incentive to maximize profit.

INTERVIEWER: You are exactly right. It turns out that CanadaCo's higher sales are due primarily to a significantly higher level of customer service. The stores are cleaner, more attractive, better stocked, and so on. The company discovered this through a series of customer surveys last year. I think you've sufficiently covered the Canadian market. Let's move now to a discussion of the U.S. market.

CANDIDATE: How many stores does USCo own in the United States, and how many does the second largest discount retailer own?

INTERVIEWER: USCo owns 4,000 stores, and the second largest competitor owns approximately 1,000 stores.

CANDIDATE: Are USCo stores bigger than those of the typical discount retailer in the United States?

INTERVIEWER: Yes. USCo stores average 200,000 square feet, whereas the typical discount retail store is approximately 100,000 square feet.

CANDIDATE: Those numbers suggest that USCo should be selling roughly eight times the volume of the nearest U.S. competitor!

INTERVIEWER: Close. USCo's sales are approximately $5 billion, whereas the nearest competitor sells about $1 billion worth of merchandise.

CANDIDATE: I would think that sales of that size give USCo significant clout with suppliers. Does it have a lower cost of goods than the competition?

INTERVIEWER: In fact, its cost of goods is approximately 15 percent less than that of the competition.

CANDIDATE: So it probably has lower prices.

INTERVIEWER: Right again. Its prices are on average about 10 percent lower than those of the competition.

CANDIDATE: So it seems that USCo has been so successful primarily because it has lower prices than its competitors.

INTERVIEWER: That's partly right. Its success probably also has something to do with a larger selection of products, given the larger average store size.

CANDIDATE: How did USCo get so much bigger than the competition?

INTERVIEWER: It started by building superstores in rural markets served mainly by mom-and-pop stores and small discount retailers. USCo bet that people would be willing to buy from it, and it was right. As it grew and developed more clout with suppliers, it began to buy out other discount retailers and convert their stores to the USCo format.

CANDIDATE: So whenever USCo buys out a competing store, it also physically expands it?

INTERVIEWER: Not necessarily. Sometimes it does, but when I said it converts it to the USCo format, I meant that it carries the same brands at prices that are on average 10 percent lower than the competition's.

CANDIDATE: What criteria does USCo use in deciding whether it should physically expand a store it's just bought out?

INTERVIEWER: It depends on a lot of factors, such as the size of the existing store, local market competition, local real estate costs, and so on, but I don't think we need to go into that here.

CANDIDATE: Well, I thought it might be relevant in terms of predicting what it will do with the 300 stores that it bought in Canada.

INTERVIEWER: Let's just assume that it doesn't plan to expand the Canadian stores beyond their current size.

CANDIDATE: OK. I think I've learned enough about USCo. I'd like to ask a few questions about USCo's ability to succeed in the Canadian market. Does USCo have a strong brand name in Canada?

INTERVIEWER: No. Although members of the Canadian business community are certainly familiar with the company because of its U.S. success, the Canadian consumer is basically unaware of USCo's existence.

CANDIDATE: Does CanadaCo carry products similar to USCo's, or does the Canadian consumer expect different products and brands than the U.S. discount retail consumer?

INTERVIEWER: The two companies carry similar products although the CanadaCo stores lean more heavily toward Canadian suppliers.

CANDIDATE: How much volume does CanadaCo actually sell?

INTERVIEWER: About $750 million worth of goods annually.

CANDIDATE: Is there any reason to think that the costs of doing business for USCo will be higher in the Canadian market?

INTERVIEWER: Can you be more specific?

CANDIDATE: I mean, for example, are labor or leasing costs higher in Canada than in the United States?

INTERVIEWER: Canada does have significantly higher labor costs, and I'm not sure about the costs of leasing space. What are you driving at?

CANDIDATE: I was thinking that if there were a higher cost of doing business in Canada, perhaps USCo would have to charge higher prices than it does in the United States to cover its costs.

INTERVIEWER: That's probably true, but remember, CanadaCo must also cope with the same high labor costs. Can you think of additional costs incurred by USCo's Canadian operations that would not be incurred by CanadaCo?

CANDIDATE: USCo might incur higher distribution costs than CanadaCo because it will have to ship product from its U.S. warehouses up to Canada.

INTERVIEWER: You are partially right. CanadaCo has the advantage in distribution costs since its network spans less geographic area and it gets more products from Canadian suppliers. However, since CanadaCo continues to get a good deal of products from the

United States, the actual advantage to CanadaCo is not great—only about 2 percent of overall costs.

CANDIDATE: All this suggests that USCo will be able to retain a significant price advantage over CanadaCo's stores: if not 10 percent, then at least 7 to 8 percent.

INTERVIEWER: I would agree with that conclusion.

The last step according to the BCG framework is to summarize and make recommendations:

CANDIDATE: I would tell the CEO the following: In the near term, you might be safe. Your stores have a much stronger brand name in Canada than USCo's, and they seem to be well managed. However, as consumers get used to seeing prices that are consistently 7 to 8 percent less at USCo, they will realize that shopping at USCo means significant savings over the course of the year. Although some consumers will remain loyal out of habit, or because of your high level of service, it is reasonable to expect the discount shopper to shop where prices are lowest. Moreover, over time your brand-name advantage will erode as USCo becomes more familiar to Canadian consumers. You certainly have to worry about losing significant share to USCo stores in the long term. You should probably do something about it now, before it's too late.

INTERVIEWER: Can you suggest possible strategies for CanadaCo?

CANDIDATE: Maybe it can find ways to cut costs and make the organization more efficient, so it can keep prices low even if its cost of goods is higher.

INTERVIEWER: Anything else?

CANDIDATE: It might consider instituting something like a frequent shopper program, where consumers accumulate points that entitle them to future discounts on merchandise.

INTERVIEWER: What might be a potential problem with that?

CANDIDATE: Well, it might not be that cost-effective since it would be rewarding a significant number of shoppers who would have continued to shop there anyway.

INTERVIEWER: Any other suggestions?

CANDIDATE: CanadaCo might want to prepare a marketing or advertising campaign that highlights its high level of service. It might even institute a CanadaCo Service Guarantee that surpasses any guarantees offered by USCo.

INTERVIEWER: Assuming the only way to keep customers is through competitive pricing, is there anything CanadaCo can do to appear competitive to the consumer?

CANDIDATE: It might want to consider offering fewer product lines, so that it can consolidate its buying power and negotiate prices with suppliers that are competitive with USCo's. It might lose some customers who want the variety of products that USCo has, but it may be able to retain the customer who is buying a limited array of items and is just looking for the best price.

123 DISCOUNT BROKERAGE REDUCING COSTS CASE

The Wellesley College Consulting Club offers students a number of practice business cases, including this one adapted from The Insider's Guide to Management Consulting: Opportunities for Undergraduates, *by Gautam Prakash, a former McKinsey & Company consultant.*

All publicly traded companies are required by law to have annual stockholder meetings in which the stockholders are asked to submit proxy votes (in person or by mail) on various resolutions. Your client is a discount brokerage firm whose main job is to count proxy votes from companies' annual stockholder meetings. It collects millions of votes by mail, tabulates the results, and then mails the results to the publicly traded company, which will then report the results to the public.

The merger mania of the 1980s helped the client grow rapidly. It expanded from one location in the Chicago suburbs to ten locations across the country, mostly located in downtown urban centers such as Wall Street in New York. Then came the 1990s.

The boom was over and suddenly the client faced falling profits. It has asked you to help reduce costs. How would you proceed? What kind of information would you need from the client? What analyses would you do? And what might your preliminary hypotheses be?

Although the interviewer invites the candidate to respond as an individual, it's psychologically astute to respond in the inclusive "we," as if the candidate were already on board. Note how the candidate builds consensus and suggests he or she is a team player:

> Let's see if we can agree on a hypothesis. As a discount brokerage that counts proxy votes, this company relies heavily on both electronic data communication (e-mail, fax, computer networks, etc.) and postal communication with its customers. While full-service brokerages need prime retail locations to serve customers, a discount broker doing business primarily through electronic communications has less need to be in prime, urban locations. Let's hypothesize we can move the company out of urban centers into suburban or even rural areas where rents (and perhaps salaries) would be reduced with no negative impact on sales. Also, the client may be able to serve its customers equally well with fewer locations. Consolidation of locations will reduce costs by reducing overhead and sharing support services. In fact, the company may also want to consider centralizing more functions at headquarters, thereby reducing the staffing level at each of the locations.
>
> One way to verify this hypothesis is to determine profitability by locations. This will require revenue and cost data for each location. Another analysis we would do is to benchmark the client's performance to other companies in the industry to see if shrinking profits is industrywide or just specific to our client. We need to validate our assumption that salaries and rents are the big cost items for this company. Determining the key factors that influence cost is important since that is where the biggest bang for the buck is. For now, let's focus initially only on ways to reduce the major cost items. To validate the assumption that location is not that important to the operations of the business, we will need to conduct customer

interviews to see what they consider important buying factors (Price? Quality of service? Face-to-face contact? Reliability of service? And so on). From the customer interview, we might also be able to separate or "segment" the discount brokerage industry into smaller pieces based on customer needs. We would then gather data on each segment to determine its size (in dollars) and growth rate. From this analysis, the client will know its strengths and weaknesses for each market segment and will know where to focus its resources to boost revenues.

124 PBX MANUFACTURER SALES STRATEGY CASE

This sales strategy business case is adapted from materials provided by the Wellesley College Consulting Club.

Consider a PBX manufacturer that designs and builds large telephone systems for offices and offers dozens of value-added features such as conference calling and voice mail. The majority of the company's sales come through direct sales by its dedicated sales force.

The PBX manufacturer has engaged you to advise it on how to make its sales force more effective. One of your analyses is to figure out how to best compensate the sales representatives. On the first day of this project you and your team brainstorm, trying to determine the key issues and analyses you need to do to answer the question. I'd like you to brainstorm for me; tell me how you would compensate the reps to make them more effective.

Listen to the instructions. The interviewer wants you to brainstorm. Remember that in brainstorming, your goal is to come up with creative solutions without, at this point, evaluating them. Here's one thoughtful response cast, for the most part, in the inclusive first person:

First, let's agree that the best way to incent salespeople is to align their success with that of the organization. That is, they make more when they sell more, and the more they sell, the more they make. A reasonable amount of greed in a sales rep is good, wouldn't you agree? Thus, a component of their pay should be incentive pay. Two issues arise out of this assumption. The first issue is how to provide the best incentives for the reps. For any given product, what is the incentive structure? Is it 5 percent of the sales price? Does it vary with the number of units sold to any given customer? To figure this out, we would want to analyze the cost structure of a product (e.g., manufacturing, freight, etc.). Given a target profit margin, the sales rep's incentive pay (which is part of the product's cost) can be "plugged" if all other elements of cost are known. That is, if we sell a product for $500 and it costs me $200 to produce and we want to make a $200 profit, then we can afford to pay the sales rep up to $100 in sales commissions. Thus, each product will have a different kind of incentive pay, determined by the other elements of cost.

The second issue to brainstorm is which products should the company provide incentives on? Are we agreed that it's generally a sound assumption to encourage reps to sell products with the highest profitability? Thus, reps should earn extra sales commission for pushing the products with the highest margins. The commission structure could become quite elaborate to maximize a company's earnings; for example, reps could earn above and beyond normal commissions for special feats, such as closing a sale quickly.

What really motivates salespeople? Cash, of course. But might there be noncash incentives? We would do well, also, to get feedback from top-performing sales reps on how to best promote salespeople. Sales prizes such as trips to Hawaii come to mind. Salespeople have big egos. Sales contests with recognition from the CEO might also be effective. Sales contests would have the additional benefit of iden-tifying our weakest performing salespeople for additional training or replacement. In any case, a complicated incentive-based pay approach may look great on paper, but fail in practice. So it's important to get people in the field (in addition to corporate management) involved since field reps often have insights into which sales and marketing tactics will actually work.

125 SELLING LAWN MOWER BUSINESS

Here's another business case described by the Wellesley College Consulting Club. Also adapted from The Insider's Guide to Management Consulting: Opportunities for Undergraduates, *by Gautam Prakash, this business case tests candidates on how to value a business.*

I have a lawn mowing business that I want to sell to your client. How would you advise your client about how to value the business for purchase?

Hint: Note that this business case asks the candidate to "consult" for the buyer, not the seller, of the business.

Fixing the value of a business is among the most difficult assignments a consultant may get. There are so many tangible and intangible variables that go into valuating a business. While it's tempting to get right into the tangible assets, it may be useful for the candidate to start with basics. Again, note how the candidate gets into the inclusive "we" voice as quickly as possible.

> Before anything else, I would sit down with my client and ask the most basic question: why do you want to get into the lawn mowing business? It's a seasonable, high-risk, highly hands-on business. If my client has no desire to manage such a business, then I would suggest the exercise of valuing the business is moot. Of course, any business has a book value—the value of its cash on hand, physical assets, accounts receivable, etc.—so perhaps my client wants to buy it for resale. The first step is to get our minds around that.
>
> Assuming that my client is determined to get into the lawn mowing business, I would say that there are two components to determining what that price would be. The first is determining the amount of profit the client could make by running the business and selling it at the end. That is, we want to understand what the business is worth in terms of cash flow and in terms of terminal value. Generally speaking, cash flow is the difference between cash put into the business and cash taken out of the business, while terminal value is the intrinsic value of the company and includes hard assets

(like the lawn mower) and intangible "goodwill" (i.e., things that you can't physically touch, like customer loyalty).

The second component to determining what price we would pay is the value the client places on his money. In economic terms, this is called the opportunity cost of capital. For example, if the client chose to keep his money in a bank CD and earn 5 percent, then his opportunity cost of capital is 5 percent since by removing his money from the bank (to pay for the lawn mowing business) he immediately loses the 5 percent interest earnings. And that doesn't even include the cost of risk.

126 NO LIGHT BEER IN THE UNITED KINGDOM

This is an international business case that does not fit with any common frameworks. It is a case used by the consulting firm Inductis, Inc., based in New Providence, New Jersey. An analysis of this case can be found at http://www.inductis.com/careers.html.

Why is there no light beer in the United Kingdom?

For this case, the best approach is to dissect the case's parts by simply listing the alternative reasons for each component of the issue. Here is one approach a recruiter at Inductis found compelling:

> The reason there is no light beer could be because (1) consumers do not demand it, (2) producers are not producing it, despite consumer demand, or (3) some outside influence, such as the government, will not permit light beer in the country. Following the producer option, one can subdivide the problem as nobody wants to sell light beer in the United Kingdom or somehow light beer producers are blocked out of the United Kingdom.

127 DONALD TRUMP'S ANSWERING MACHINE CASE

This is an example of a "What would Croesus do?" problem. Croesus was a legendary rich guy. The issue is deciding how a person with unlimited resources would approach a problem and then taking lessons from that to design something more affordable. By asking a design question in this way, we, too, become smarter and richer.

How would Donald Trump (or any other individual with nearly unlimited resources) prevent being disturbed at night by a wrong number? How can we use that information to design a solution accessible to consumers without such resources?

The obvious answer is to outsource the problem. The easiest solution is for Donald Trump to hire someone (perhaps the winner of his reality TV show, *The Apprentice*) to answer his phone 24 hours a day. If the call were a wrong number or a fax machine, Trump's assistant, not he, would deal with the problem.

When you come up with an answer, you're not done. You know that a solution exists, but the problem with Donald Trump's solution is that it will be too expensive to be practical. Turning the Trump solution into something practical still requires a good deal of effort. The second step is to think of ways to make this solution more affordable. How could we standardize or automate the services of a personal assistant? Calls could be directed to an answering service. Most doctors use this approach, but it's still too expensive to be a general solution for most consumers.

Could the screening be done by a machine? One option is to create a list of approved numbers that would be able to get through. This is called a white list. While this solves most of the problem, it would be a good deal of work to compile a list of approved numbers and maintain it. Consumers would always worry that the list would be incomplete. An alternative to the approved list is the use of a code. Preferred callers could be given a code to input to get the phone to ring through. But making phone calls could get a bit complicated when every phone number also has a code.

Another solution is a screening device that screens out calls from specific telephone numbers. This is called a black list. Again, such a list would be very difficult to create and maintain and would not protect Trump from unwanted calls from numbers not on the black list.

Think for a moment about these two machine-screening approaches. The approved number list creates a screen at the receiving end, whereas the code pushes the screen out to the caller. The caller has the advantage of being smarter than a machine. Make the code something obvious, like "0." If we just give the caller the right information, the person can use discretion. Thus we return to the message: "You've reached the Trumps. We're home but don't wish to be disturbed right now. If this is an emergency, you can hit '0' and our phone will ring. But it had better be good."

The first part of the message prevents wrong numbers. The second part allows the caller to self-screen. Perhaps the irony of this solution is that while it would be 99-percent effective for most of us, it wouldn't work very well for the Trumps.

GROSS ORDER OF ESTIMATION PROBLEMS

Gross order of estimation problems, also known as market-sizing problems or Fermi Problems, are designed to gauge how comfortable candidates are with numbers and whether they can quickly zero in on market drivers, make reasonable assumptions, and work through to a defensible guesstimate. Usually, the interviewer neither knows the answer to the question nor cares about it. Rather, the interviewer wishes to see the candidate "light up" with enthusiasm for the challenge and to display a logical process for reaching some kind of answer.

"Smart candidates will realize that you are not quizzing them on their knowledge, and they will enthusiastically leap into trying to figure out some back-of-the-envelope answer," says Fog Creek Software's Joel Spolsky. One of the puzzles he sometimes asks is, How many gas stations are there in Los Angeles? Then he listens closely. "Smart candidates will be methodical," Spolsky says. "'Well, let's see, the population of LA is about 7 million; each adult in LA has about 2.5 cars . . . ' Of course it's OK if they are radically wrong. The important thing is that they leapt into the question enthusiastically. They may try to figure out the capacity of a gas station. 'Gee, it takes four minutes to tank up, gas stations have about 10 pumps and are open about 18 hours a day . . . ' They may try to figure it out by area. Sometimes they will surprise you with their creativity or ask for a Los Angeles yellow pages. All good signs.

CHAPTER 9

"Not-so-smart candidates will get flustered and upset. They will just stare at you like you landed from Mars. You have to coach them. 'Well, if you were building a new city the size of Los Angeles, how many gas stations would you put in it?' You can give them little hints. 'How long does it take to fill up a tank of gas?' Still, with not-so-smart candidates, you will have to drag them along while they sit there stupidly and wait for you to rescue them. These people are not problem solvers, and we don't want them working for us."

Remember, the number you calculate is meaningless; the calculation is always more interesting. The interviewer only wants to see your thinking process. Of course, if your conclusions are widely off, the interviewers may raise their eyebrows. But there are many ways to come up with an answer. You would really impress the interviewer after you're done if you offered to recalculate the answer using a different method and then explained possible sources of error in your calculations!

A word about Fermi problems. Fermi problems receive their name from Enrico Fermi (1901–1954), an Italian-born physicist known for his participation in the Manhattan Project (the atomic bomb project) and the development of quantum theory. Fermi problems emphasize estimation, numerical reasoning, communication in mathematics, and questioning skills. Candidates often believe that "word problems" have one exact answer and that the answer is derived in a unique manner. Fermi problems encourage multiple approaches, emphasize process rather than "the answer," and promote nontraditional problem-solving strategies. More than 40 additional Fermi problems are listed in Appendix C.

Note that although every estimation puzzle in this chapter, like the others in this book, culminates with a "solution" statement, it merely summarizes the results of the particular calculation selected for the estimation. The solutions are not intended to suggest that other estimations, even yielding wildly different results, may not be equally valid. The solutions are certainly not intended to suggest that the values have any basis in reality.

As they say in TV ads, actual results may vary.

128 MANHATTAN PAY PHONES

This is one of the classic estimation problems favored by Microsoft and Hewlett-Packard.

How many pay phones are there on the island of Manhattan?

Hint: Think of Manhattan as a grid.

A logical place to begin your analysis might be to ballpark the number of Manhattan street corners. If you think of New York City as a grid of streets, you might guess it is about 300 streets long by 10 avenues wide, so it has approximately 3,000 intersections. You might then assume there are 2 pay phones for every intersection, for a total of about 6,000 pay phones.

Solution: 6,000 pay phones.

Extra credit: Subtract the number of intersections that are invalidated because they fall in the area of Central Park. Say Central Park is 30 blocks long by 3 blocks wide, or 90 intersections. Using your 2-pay-phones-for-every-intersection assumption, you would want to subtract 180 pay phones from the original 6,000. You might then add to the 5,820 the number of pay phones that might be found in restaurants, hotels, schools, hospitals, and office building lobbies. How would you calculate that figure?

More extra credit: Mention that a combination of forces—the market penetration of cell phones and the fight against terrorism and the drug trade—has drastically reduced the number of pay phones.

129 SHAMPOO AND CONDITIONER

This puzzle turns up in college interviews by both McKinsey & Company and Boston Consulting Group.

How many hotel-size bottles of shampoo and conditioner are produced each year around the world?

You might begin by assuming that hotel-size bottles are produced for two purposes only:

1. To supply hotels and upscale motels
2. To provide samples for gift packs, salons, etc.

You would then want to start by estimating the number of hotels and motels around the world that offer the products to their guests. One way of estimating the number of hotels around the world is to assume that hotels are found predominantly in major cities and resort towns. Figure that there are 2,000 major cities and resorts around the world, an average of 10 for each of the world's approximately 200 countries. Assume that each city averages 20 hotels that offer bottled hair products to their guests. Multiplying 20 by 2,000 gives you 40,000 hotels around the world that require shampoo and/or conditioner for their guests.

To understand how many bottles of shampoo and conditioner the 40,000 hotels require, you now need to estimate the total number of uses that each hotel on average represents. You can arrive at that number through the following calculation: Assume that there are 100 rooms in each hotel and that those rooms are occupied 50 percent of the time. Multiplying 40,000 by 100 by 0.5 by 365 (don't forget the number of days in the year!) gives you approximately 750 million.

Solution: About 750 million.

Extra credit: It is probably reasonable to assume that a guest staying for longer than a day will not use a whole shampoo bottle every day. If you assume that an average of one shampoo bottle is used for every two occupied days in a given room, you can now divide your estimate of 750 million in half to 375 million.

To get to the number of bottles of conditioner, estimate a ratio between the use of shampoo and the use of conditioner. Since many of us do not condition every time we shampoo, you might assume that the ratio is 2:1. Dividing 375 million in half gives you approximately 190 million. Your conclusion would then be that 375 million bottles of shampoo and 190 million bottles of conditioner are required for hotel use every year.

To estimate the total market size, you can probably make things easy on yourself by assuming that the number produced for sample purposes is a small percentage of the total, say 10 percent. Combining your two markets would give you approximately 400 million bottles of shampoo and 210 million bottles of conditioner.

Finally, you might want to "reality-check" your total figure. Assuming 610 million bottles are produced and sold each year at an average price of

25 cents each, the worldwide market for miniature bottles of shampoo and conditioner is about $150 million. Does that sound reasonable?

Solution: 400 million bottles of shampoo and 210 million bottles of conditioner.

130 SUGAR CONSUMPTION IN AMERICA

A number of candidates report that consulting firms in the Midwest have used this puzzle or variants of it, such as how many pounds of potatoes does the average American consume in a year?

How much sugar does the average American consume in a year?

This estimation problem was offered by a consulting firm that serves the processed foods industry. The recruiter found the following response very appealing because the candidate actually found a data point in real time from which to begin:

> Let's start by gathering facts before making assumptions. I'm going to try to calculate the amount of sugar by the number of calories the average American consumes. Thankfully, you were good enough to offer me a can of Pepsi. Looking at the Nutrition Facts on the can, I determine that the can of Pepsi contains 43 grams of sugar and yields 160 calories. Thus, we calculate that there are 3.7 calories per gram of sugar. Now, I assume that the average American consumes 2,500 calories per day. Assuming that sugars account for 25 percent of those calories, the average American consumes 168 grams of sugar per day. Converting to pounds, we divide by 454 grams per pound to yield 0.37 pounds of sugar per day. Multiplying by 365 days per year brings us to 135 pounds of sugar per American per year.

Solution: 135 pounds of sugar per year.

Another candidate took a much simpler approach to yield a surprisingly close result:

> I'm going to begin by assuming that the average American consumes one cup of sugar per day. Now, one cup of sugar is about 6 ounces.

That means the average American consumes 2,190 ounces of sugar over the course of a year. Converting to pounds, we get 137 pounds of sugar per year.

Extra credit: As a reality check, a quick visit to the American Sugar Council's Web site yields this statistic: the average American consumes about 150 pounds of sugar per year. Sweet.

Solution: 137 pounds per year.

131 DISPOSABLE DIAPER CONSUMPTION

This puzzle was used by Bain & Company recruiters when they interviewed at the Wharton School, University of Pennsylvania, and the Stern School of Business, New York University.

How many infant disposable diapers were sold in the United States last year?

In answering this question, all you have to work with are assumptions. If you are unsure about an assumption or unsure about what is being requested of you, do not hesitate to ask questions of the interviewer. The best interviews are conversations, not Q&A sessions. Here is one candidate's take on the disposable diaper estimation:

I am going to assume that the population of the United States is 300 million people. I am going to further assume that the average life expectancy in the United States is 75 years. For simplicity's sake, I am also going to assume that there are an equal number of people in each age group. So 300 million people divided by 75 different age groups equals 4 million people in each age group. Children wear diapers from age zero to age three, so that's 3 years. Four million children times 3 years equals 12 million. Out of those 12 million children, I am going to assume that 80 percent of them wear disposable diapers. That's 9.6 million children. Let's also assume that the average child goes through five diapers a day. Newborns maybe more than five, three-year-olds maybe less, so we will assume five diapers a day. 9.6 million kids times five diapers a day equals 48 million diapers a day. So 48 million diapers a day times 365 days a year is your answer.

Extra credit: Mention the fact that the market for *adult* disposable diapers represents another important opportunity.

132 PIANO TUNERS IN THE UNITED STATES

This is a favorite gross order estimation problem at Microsoft. Again, the interviewer doesn't know or care about the answer. The interviewer wants to see how the candidate reframes the gross order of estimation question, breaks it down, and communicates a rational solution.

How many piano tuners are there in the United States?

Ole Eichorn, on his blog called *The Critical Connection* (http://w-uh.com/), takes a crack at the puzzle like this:

> This is one of those questions which doesn't have a "right" answer; nobody really knows the answer, and you probably can't Google to find it. But there is a way to come up with a reasonable estimate, and this is obviously what the interviewer wants you to do. Plugging in the "right" numbers is not nearly as important as coming up with the approach. If you gave the following schema for computing an answer, the interviewer would be pleased:
>
> 1. Estimate the number of people in the United States.
> 2. Estimate how many of them own pianos.
> 3. Estimate how many "other" pianos there are.
> 4. Estimate how long it takes to tune a piano.
> 5. Estimate how often a piano needs tuning.
> 6. Using the data from steps 4 and 5, estimate how many piano tuners there are per piano.
> 7. Using the data from steps 2, 3, and 6, estimate how many piano tuners there are in the United States.

If a candidate actually wants to generate an estimate rather than just articulating a schema, the following approach is sound:

> Let's assume there are 75 million families in the United States, and 10 percent have pianos. That's 7.5 million pianos. Each piano needs to be tuned once a year. Now, let's assume the average piano tuner can tune 4 pianos a day. That means the average piano tuner, working 300 days a year, can tune 1,200 pianos a year. Doing the division, I'd say there are 6,250 piano tuners in the United States.

Solution: 6,250 piano tuners.

133 CARS IN THE UNITED STATES

This is a frequently asked puzzle at Microsoft, either in this form or in the form of the next gross order of estimation problem. In any case, the analysis of the following problem requires most candidates to first tackle this one.

How many cars are there in the United States?

Most candidates start by stating their assumption of the population of the United States. It's not absolutely critical to get that statistic right, but it helps. It happens to be around 300 million. The second step is to make an assumption about the percentage of Americans who own cars. As long as you're making assumptions, now's a good time to assume away. For example, list the categories of people who do not own cars: prisoners, children, the homeless, many residents of Manhattan, etc. You might mention that you recognize that some individuals own more than one car. Mention whether you will count or ignore "fleet" cars owned by car rental agencies, etc. If you're really careful, you can consider the cars that are sitting, not yet owned, at the nation's car dealers. Let's say you will ignore fleet cars and unsold inventory. Unless you have a sound basis for another assumption—why make this harder than it should be?—most interviewers will be satisfied if you pick a reasonable percentage. For our purposes, let's say that 65 percent of this car-obsessed country owns a car. In that case, a reasonable estimate is 195 million cars in the United States.

Solution: 195 million cars.

134 GAS STATIONS IN THE UNITED STATES

Another guesstimation question very popular at Microsoft.

How many gas stations are there in the United States?

The first order of business is to estimate the number of cars in the United States (see the problem above). There are many creative ways to solve this market-sizing problem, but let's stick to the traditional method. It may be boring, but it has the least chance of making you look foolish. The first step is to state to the interviewer the approach you intend to take. Here's how one candidate explained it:

> The way I intend to solve this problem is to estimate how many cars there are in the United States and how many cars per day the average gas station can service. By dividing the former number by the latter, I believe we will have an estimate of the number of gas stations in the United States.

We are operating under the assumption that there are 195 million cars in the United States. The next piece of the puzzle to calculate is the frequency of fueling. You can use your own experience as the basis of this assumption. Let's say for the sake of argument you fuel up once per week. That means that in the span of a week, the nation's gas stations service the equivalent of all the cars in the country, 195 million cars.

The next order of business is to estimate the number of cars a gas station can handle in a week. Once you can calculate the productivity of the average gas station, it is a simple matter to calculate the number of gas stations. Here you can take a shortcut or make it hard on yourself. The problem is to estimate how many hours per week the typical gas station is open. It's true that not all service stations are open 24-7. If that is your assumption, you have to make a correction. But more and more gas stations are open 24-7. With unattended self-service and all-night gas stations proliferating, it's reasonable to assume that all stations are available 24 hours per day, 7 days per week.

How long does it take to fill up a car? Considering the time it takes to wait for the credit card authorization or go inside to pay, let's assume it takes 10 minutes to fill up the average car. At this point, it is useful to state that the one-pump gas station is pretty much obsolete. Most gas stations, in fact, have 10, 20, or even more pumps. On the other hand, there are still many remote gas stations where hours can pass between customers. There is little to do but make another assumption: let's say that the average gas station fuels up 10 cars per hour.

Now we can do the math. The average gas station fuels up $24 \cdot 7 \cdot 10$, or 1,680 cars per week. That means there are $195,000,000/1,680 = 116,071$ gas stations.

Solution: 116,071 gas stations.

Reality check: National Department of Transportation Statistics (U.S. Department Transportation) reported 129,748,704 registered passenger vehicles in the United States in 2001. According to the National Association of Convenience Stores, there are 120,000 retail sites selling motor fuel in the United States.

135 GOLF BALL CONSUMPTION

Golf, for some reason, appears to be the subject of fascination at both McKinsey & Company and Bain & Company, where candidates have reported facing this question.

How many golf balls are manufactured in the United States, and what factors drive demand?

A former Bain & Company recruiter remembers the following response as one of the best he received for this challenge:

> Let's see, I don't play golf, but I believe that golf ball sales are driven by end users. So let's determine a reasonable number of logical prospects that are in the golf ball market. This will be some fraction of the total U.S. population, which is about 300 million. If I can assume a uniform age distribution and an average life expectancy of 80 years,

I estimate that only people in the ages 20–70 will be logical prospects. Thus I can eliminate 30 of 80 years, or ⅜ of the 300 million population. That means the market is reduced to a potential buyer pool of about 110 million. But not all of those play golf. Based on my experience, I'd say 4 out of 10 people play golf. So now ⁴⁄₁₀ of 110 million gets us down to 44 million people who play golf and buy golf balls.

Now let's estimate frequency of purchase, specifically how many golf balls an average consumer buys per month.

Based on the golf ball packaging at the retail level, I am going to assume that the average golfer buys 3 golf balls per month. So demand is 3 · 44 million, or 132 million per month. Finally, we need to estimate the number of months per year that people play golf. Twelve months in places like Florida; maybe four months in states with cold weather. Let's do an average and decide that eight months a year is a reasonable estimate. So that allows us to calculate 8 · 132 million, or 1.1 billion golf balls per year.

Solution: 1.1 billion golf balls.

Extra credit: Refine the average purchase assumption by considering that retired people play golf much more than working professionals.

136 TOOTH FAIRY DISTRIBUTION
A fun estimation puzzle that nevertheless welcomes some deep analytical insights.

How much money does the tooth fairy distribute worldwide each year?

At times the puzzle is framed something like this: The tooth fairy has asked us to submit a bid to manage the global tooth fairy franchise contract. Ignoring administration, transportation, wages, etc., calculate the capital reserve we will need the first year to pay out the tooth fairy obligation at a rate of $0.25 per tooth.

A recruiter at a Fortune 500 company who uses this puzzle recalls this response as close to ideal:

Correct me if I'm wrong. What you are looking for is the number of payouts at 25 cents the company would have in the first year under this contract.

The candidate pauses to make sure the question he or she will address is the right one and then continues:

Well, people lose teeth every day, but let's focus on children who are 10 years old or younger because that population is the tooth fairy's natural market. I'm assuming there are 6 billion people in the world with an average life span of 60 years, so one-tenth of the population is 10 years or under. That's 600 million kids. Let's ignore population growth. Now, each child has 20 baby teeth (adults have 32 teeth, but that's another story). That means we are talking about 12 little incisors and premolars.

So in the worst-case scenario, if every child lost every tooth the first year, our obligation would be $3 billion. If we assume that the loss of teeth is evenly distributed among the 10 years of a child's life, a reasonable sense of the tooth fairy's obligation in the first year is 10 percent of $3 billion, or $300 million.

But I would reconsider this contract, because at a payout of $0.25 per tooth, we would get our pants sued off by the first kid for breach of implied contract. Some of these kids have their lawyer's name on speed dial.

Solution: $300 million the first year.

137 BARBERS IN THE UNITED STATES

This puzzle turns up from time to time at companies as diverse as Hewlett-Packard, Amazon, and McKinsey & Company.

How many barbers are there in the United States?

As always, start with some assumptions: Barbers service only boys and men. There are about 300 million people in the United States, and half of them are men, so there are 150 million men in the United States. But babies and toddlers generally don't go to barbers. So we're dealing with 80 percent of the population, or 120 million people. Let's say each of them gets a haircut once a month. That's 120 million haircuts a month.

Now let's consider how many people a barber can serve in a typical shift. Let's assume a barber can perform a haircut in 15 minutes, or 4 per hour. That's 160 haircuts in a 40-hour week. Some barbers work less, some work more, but 160 haircuts a week, or 640 haircuts per month, seems reasonable. Thus 120 million people divided by 640 gives 187,500 barbers.

Solution: 187,500 barbers.

138 ICE HOCKEY WEIGHT

This puzzle is representative of a class of physics-intensive estimation challenges in which some technical knowledge of the properties of matter, in this case, water and ice, are definitely helpful. Often problems in this category ask for the weight of some really bulky item. Accenture favors this question in its interviews for consultants and project managers.

What does all the ice in a hockey rink weigh?

The first task is to decide whether to solve this problem in English (pounds) or metric (kilograms) units. For a very good reason, as we will see, using the metric system is preferred. The first step is to calculate the area of a hockey rink. Let's say it's 100 by 200 feet, or (1 foot = 0.30 meter) approximately 30 by 60 meters, or 3,000 by 6,000 centimeters. Let's also assume the ice is 2.5 centimeters thick. That gives us 45 million cubic centimeters of ice.

How much does a cubic centimeter of ice weigh? Well, we know that by definition, a cubic centimeter of water weighs 1 gram. (This is why the metric system is preferred. Quick! What does a cubic inch of water weigh?) Ice weighs a little less than water, but for this problem, we can assume they weigh the same. So we are working with 45,000 kilograms of ice. Converting to pounds gives 99,000 pounds.

Solution: 99,000 pounds.

Extra credit: What if the interviewer points out that an NHL regulation ice rink is an oval, 85 by 200 feet, with a corner radius of 28 feet? Here the best solution is to calculate the weight of volume of liquid water. The math (omitted here) comes out to 38,500 kilograms, or 84,877 pounds, of water.

139 EARRING WEARERS IN THE UNITED STATES

This is a challenge that many candidates find fun because it combines estimating skills with making some educated guesses about social trends.

How many people in the United States wear earrings?

Here is another gross order of estimation question posed by Inductis. Again, no one at Inductis knows or cares what the actual number is. The only criteria are whether the candidate can arrive at a reasonable figure, articulate it, and defend the analysis. An awareness of social trends is a help. Here is an analysis that an Inductis recruiter would find familiar:

There are approximately 300 million people in the United States.

Of those, about ½ are women.

Of the 150 million women, ⅘ are adults.

Of the 120 million adult women, about ¾ wear either pierced or clip-on earrings, for a total of 90 million people.

Of the 30 million girls, about ⅘ wear earrings by the time they are 15, making 24 million girls.

Now, since more and more men wear earrings, let's consider men. Of the 150 million men, ⅘ are adults.

Of the 120 million adult men, about ¹⁄₂₀ wear earrings (based on my personal experience), for a total of 7.5 million.

Of the 30 million boys, only about ¹⁄₅₀ have parents who will let them wear earrings, for a total of 0.6 million boys.

Adding up all the constituencies for wearing earrings, the estimate is that 122.1 million people in the United States wear earrings.

Solution: 122.1 million people.

140 QUARTER COINS IN YANKEE STADIUM

This is another gross order of estimation problem favored by Inductis recruiters.

How many quarter coins are there in Yankee Stadium during a sold-out baseball game?

According to a recruiting training guide issued by Inductis, the following assumptions and analysis are standard for this puzzler:

> Yankee Stadium holds approximately 50,000 fans.
>
> There are approximately 150 additional people working at the stadium.
>
> Of the workers, each of them either carry approximately 40 quarters or have 40 in their cash registers to provide change to customers, for a total of 6,000 quarters.
>
> Of the fans, approximately four-fifths are male.
>
> Of that 40,000, half are like my dad and have about 10 quarters in their pockets at any given time, for a total of 200,000 quarters.
>
> Of the remaining 20,000, half have no quarters, and half have 6 quarters to ride the subway home, for a total of 60,000 quarters.
>
> Of the 10,000 women, half have 12 quarters for themselves and their husbands or boyfriends to ride the subway home, and half have 1 quarter to call someone in an emergency, for a total of 65,000 quarters.
>
> For a grand total of 331,000 quarters in Yankee Stadium.

Solution: 331,000 quarters.

Extra credit: The above problem is clearly out of date. For extra credit, analyze how the increasing use of credit and debit cards, prepaid rapid transit cards, and cell phones, along with the general trend toward a cashless society, reduces the need for quarters to buy refreshments, pay subway fares, or make telephone calls, respectively.

141 CREDIT CARDS IN THE WORLD

Another problem featured on the Inductis (www.inductis.com/careers.html) career page.

How many credit cards are there in the world?

A standard analysis is:

> There are approximately 6 billion people in the world.
>
> Let's assume that half live in areas where they cannot get credit cards (rural areas, poverty-stricken areas, etc.).
>
> Of the 3 billion people remaining, let's assume three-fourths are adults (in the United States it's four-fifths, but we have a slower birth rate than many other countries).
>
> Of the 2.4 billion adults, one-third don't carry credit cards (they have bad credit, don't believe in credit cards, are unemployed, etc.).
>
> Of the 1.6 billion adults who carry credit cards, some have ten cards while others have just one. Let's assume each person carries an average of three cards (Visa, MasterCard, American Express).
>
> Resulting in 4.7 billion credit cards in the world.

Solution: 4.7 billion credit cards.

PERFORMANCE PUZZLES

The problems in this section are brainteasers to be acted out. They all involve an aspect of performance. Sell this; deconstruct that; design the other thing. Formerly labeled "stress" questions, these challenges are less about seeing how candidates react to stress than about seeing how they perform under stress. In any case, it's not about stress. These brainteasers invite candidates to show another aspect of their creative, engaging personalities. Not all candidates will shine in these challenges, and that's okay, but it's also okay for interviewers to know that. The key is that for these problems, many interviewers expect a real performance. They may be explicit about it and invite you up to the whiteboard. Or the interviewer can let the room fill with silence while you try to figure out what the interviewer wants. In any case, don't be afraid to role play or act out.

142 SELL ME THIS PEN

For sales positions, at least, this is perhaps the oldest performance question in job interview history. The interviewer points to a pen, a coffee mug, a stapler. It hardly matters. The interviewer says, "Sell this to me." This task tests not only a candidate's raw promotional ability—particularly useful if the position involves sales—but his or her ability to reconceptualize—the imagination required to repurpose a device or technology to new uses. Recruiters expect candidates to ask questions, but not too many questions. "I tolerate one or two questions, but then I say, 'you'd better start selling me,'" says Ed Milano, vice president of Marketing and Program Development at Design Continuum.

Please take this pen and sell it to me. Tell me about its design excellence, features, benefits, and values.

The goal here is to win the interviewer's confidence by showing your spontaneity and creativity. It's always good to focus more on the benefits to the consumer than the features of the product. Most interviewers look for a bid for action or hard close, that is, the candidate actually asking the customer for the order. Here's a traditional if conservative response. Note the hard close at the end:

> Sir, I would like to thank you for seeing me today. The reason I stopped by is I wanted to let you know about this special pen offer. My company has produced this pen for 20 years, and as you know, it is the quintessential business pen. My company has recently acquired a machine that can fashion in stainless steel your company's logo right here, and I think that pen would be used with pride by your employees and clients. And because we are introducing this new concept, we can let you take advantage of an introductory offer with an investment of $10 per unit when you order 1,000 or more. How do you feel about getting such a fine symbol of your company's success at such a fine price? How many should we order for you?

Jeffrey Yamaguchi, who runs a blog called *Working for the Man* (www.workingfortheman.com), offers this pair of responses to the "sell me this pen" challenge. The first is another conventional response:

> This is an extraordinary pen that makes writing, whether you are penning a letter to a friend or just paying bills, a truly remarkable experience. With barely any pressure to the paper at all, the pen dispenses a fine, consistent amount of ink, thereby helping to prevent strain in the hand for even the longest of writing sessions. This pen will never leak, and therefore can be carried around without any threat of ink stains on clothing. The pen is handsomely designed, as you can see. It's versatile and would be appropriate in the office or at home in that drawer where the phone books are kept. And lastly, the price is right. So how about giving this pen a try?

For those frustrated—or worse—by having to perform in job interviews, Yamaguchi offers a subversive alternative that is bound to get a laugh right before the interviewer calls security:

Well, this pen is just a regular old pen. I'm not quite sure why you would want to purchase this particular pen over other pens. There are a lot of pens to choose from in the world, and I'd just like to be honest and point out that since I've never used the pen, I can't recommend this one over the other pens available. But having been asked to do this extremely stupid little exercise, I can now honestly say that there is one particular reason for getting a hold of this pen. I'm speaking from experience, now, so you can feel quite comfortable taking my word as truth. If you happen to be job hunting in the near future, and during job interviews you are asked stupid questions by an interviewer, perhaps asked to present a hypothetical sales pitch on something that you've never seen before and have no interest in whatsoever, you could uncap this pen, grip it like you're trying to stir through thick cookie dough, and use it to stab your interviewer right in the eye. A whole bunch of times, really quickly. The sharp point on this pen right here will maximize clean, swift entries and exits, and enhance the precision of the continuous blows. Why don't you lean forward and get a little closer so that you can get a real good look at the exquisitely sharp tip of this pen . . .

143 DECONSTRUCT THIS PDA

This is an important variation of the "sell this to me" challenge. Here the issue becomes an aspect of marketing perhaps even more important than selling: understanding what you are selling. The instruction to "deconstruct" offers candidates wide latitude. In general, it means consider the constituent elements of the product, especially the opportunities to repurpose those elements to create new value. Here creativity and imagination are definitely rewarded.

Here's a personal digital assistant (PDA). Deconstruct it for me.

The interviewer can just as easily hand the candidate a cell phone, digital camera, or other nontrivial device. What the interviewer is watching for is the ability to conceptually articulate the functional elements of a device. Many approaches are possible. Some candidates talk about the physical components: the keyboard is for data entry; the LCD is for data display, etc. Ed Milano, vice president of Marketing and Program Development at Design Continuum, recalls one candidate who took his PDA, turned it on, and for five minutes silently analyzed the data it contained. Then the candidate put the PDA down and said, "This is the tool you use to manage the intersection of your personal and work lives." And then he went through all the functions—calendar, contacts, e-mail, notes—and how they would help Milano manage and preserve the boundaries.

144 MICROWAVE OVEN

A design question still popular at Microsoft. This puzzle is an open invitation to be stupid. Resist the invitation and focus on what the interviewer is really looking for.

How would you design a computer-controlled microwave oven?

Most interviewers will not be impressed by pie-in-the-sky creativity here. Rather, the focus is on the benefits of making the microwave oven just a little bit smarter. For all design questions, interviewers want to hear your plans for a focus group to identify possible benefits and consumer studies to evaluate proposed solutions. After that, it's best to stick to a handful of reasonable solutions. Interviewers also perk up their ears when they hear you speculate about what needs to happen beyond the immediate problem to really leverage the device.

Perhaps the most sensible use for a computer-controlled microwave oven is that it would be able to exploit smart packaging on food products. Under this scenario, many food items will have special preparation instructions encapsulated in a bar code or intelligent chip that would be scanned by the microwave oven. In some cases, the instructions could be downloaded from a central site. The computer would issue instructions to the oven for power levels and time settings for the defrosting and cooking stages. In any case, the consumer would be relieved of the chore of programming the microwave oven.

Extra credit: Note that the computer could maintain historical usage logs of the food products prepared. These logs would be of value to consumers who are interested in tracking information about calories or nutrition or who simply want a baseline from which to prepare shopping lists. But such information would also be of enormous value to the food industry and to companies like Microsoft that provide the data mining tools to extract knowledge from the microwave oven history logs.

What if the interviewer responds, "Smart packaging is well and good for prepared food items such as a frozen pizza. But what about when it comes to cooking a home-cooked lasagna or a piece of fresh fish?" In response, the candidate might mention that the computer would feature voice-recognition software. The system would also be able to weigh the food item on its rotating tray. Now the consumer would simply tell the microwave what was being cooked and the system would download heating instructions from a central site, correct the instructions for the precise weight of the food, and while it's at it, also adjust for altitude.

145 SPICE RACK FOR A BLIND PERSON

For some reason, this puzzle is a favorite of Microsoft recruiters. Thousands of candidates have fielded it. No two people have given the same answer. That richness of the puzzle is what makes it a favorite.

Design a spice rack for a blind person.

This is not a trivial problem, and the solution, whatever it turns out to be, is less important than the candidate's ability to define—perhaps redefine—the problem and its constraints. "For starters," says a former Microsoft recruiter, "we want to hear the candidate begin with something like, 'Okay, the goal here is to design an integrated spice storage and dispensing system that is friendly for blind people to use, is that right?'" To many recruiters, it's a plus for candidates to check if their understanding of the problem is correct.

Some recruiters want the candidates to suggest some intentional interaction with blind people instead of assuming they know what the issues for blind people are. Others give candidates extra credit if they can get beyond the conventional form factor of a spice rack and propose an innovative package. After that, recruiters want to hear the candidate consider the components of the problem (jars, lids, labeling, organizing system) and how each interrelates to the needs of the target consumer. Most candidates specify labels in Braille. After that the answers can take a variety of directions. The issue is can the candidate articulate a solution, and what happens when the recruiter challenges the design? Does the candidate immediately agree with the recruiter, or does the candidate defend his or her conception?

"This is a difficult challenge, and when it comes right down to it, the question is already steering you in the wrong direction," says Ron Jacobs, product manager for the Platform Architecture Guidance Team at Microsoft. "The goal is not the spice rack design but rather how to help a blind person quickly organize, locate, and use spices while allowing the manufacturers to label spices with Braille easily. Candidates often take this kind of question in the wrong direction, focusing narrowly on the spice rack, where better candidates think out of the box."

"Creative candidates will often surprise the interviewer with an interesting, nonobvious answer," agrees Joel Spolsky, who, when he was at Microsoft, asked the spice rack question of hundreds of candidates. "Inevitably, candidates will put Braille somewhere on the spice bottles, and it usually winds up being on top of the lid. I had one candidate who decided that it would be better to put the spices in a drawer, because it is more comfortable to scan Braille with your fingertips horizontal than vertical. (Try it!) This was so creative it surprised me—in dozens of interviews, I had never heard that answer. And it really took a major creative leap outside of the bounds of the problem. On the strength of that answer alone, and no negatives, I hired the candidate, who went on to be one of the best program managers on the Excel team," he says.

146 TESTING A SALTSHAKER

Microsoft asks lots of testing questions to determine whether candidates are aware that multiple criteria apply in evaluating even the simplest artifacts. For this question, Microsoft interviewers look for candidates who question assumptions and see things from novel perspectives. Sometimes an actual saltshaker will be produced for this puzzle.

Here's a saltshaker. Show me how you would test it.

The operative word is *show*. The recruiter is not looking for profound originality here, but is looking for more than words. This is a variety of the deconstruction puzzle with a call to action. Does the candidate understand the functions of a saltshaker and how it is used? If so, the evaluation will be broken down into logical steps. For example, what could go wrong with a saltshaker? Does the saltshaker really contain salt? Some saltshakers—especially those in many fourth-grade cafeterias—contain sugar. The candidate now tastes the contents. Is the top on securely, a design flaw common in high school lunchrooms? Test the top. Are the holes sufficient for dispensing the right amount of salt? Do the test. Is it too hard to refill? Do the test. Once you outline several levels of criteria, you could have a focus group test a variety of shakers in different realistic situations to see which designs work best.

It's critical to show that your main concern is understanding what the customer expects from the saltshaker. Unless you demonstrate that knowledge, you will not be able to verify that the tests satisfy these needs. Using inclusive language to its maximum effect, here's one candidate's preamble to the question:

> Now that I'm asked to test this saltshaker, my first question is, "What is the user need for this product?" The second question is, "How will our customers use this product to satisfy these needs, and what are the most important aspects of this usage?" There is a subtle difference in the two questions. The first question is used at a basic level to verify that we have designed something that serves the purpose the product is intended to serve. The second question is designed to make us think about how people with different work styles will leverage and care about the feature/product set we are attempting to test. While we will indeed want to think about how 80 percent of customers will use the product from point A to point B; if our focus is on testing we need to go beyond this to understand the realistic needs of someone who might want to stop at point C along the way.

Extra credit: Pepper your response with concepts such as exploratory testing, code coverage, complexity metrics, focus groups, manual testing, and automated testing.

147 HEAD SWEEP

The urban legend in the training field is that Bill Gates once gave his management new hires a brainteaser called "head sweep." The challenge went like this:

I'm going to ask you to turn your head completely to your left and then sweep from left to right only once, looking for everything in your field of vision that is blue. Once you have swept your head, please look down and do not look up again until the exercise is over.

[Candidate does so.]

Now, as you are looking down, please pick up your pen and without looking up, please write down everything that you saw that was . . . green.

The object is to determine if the candidate noted any of the colors on objects in the room that were *not* blue! How conscious is the candidate? How resistant is the candidate to tunnel vision? Bill Gates presumably believes that there may be green opportunities for improvement, but because candidates are looking only for blue solutions, they do not see the green ones.

148 TESTING A STAPLER

Another Microsoft favorite. Often the interviewer will hand the candidate a stapler just before posing the challenge.

How would you test the functionality of this stapler?

The interviewer just wants to see how many creative ways you can test the stapler. Here are some of the issues that candidates have raised:

- The length of the staples inside. If they are long, then you can staple thick documents.

- The length from the hinge to the head of the stapler. If it's long, then you can staple the center part of a document such as a pamphlet.

- How many staples can it hold at once? More is always better until the point of diminishing returns.

- Is it electronic? Do you have to exert manual pressure? How much?

- Can you unhinge the stapler so it can be used like a makeshift staple gun to attach things to walls, for example?

- Does it staple every time, or does it sometimes mess up? Let's test it.

- What other uses might it have? Paperweight? Clamp?

- Does it have a warranty?

Vikas Hamine, a graduate student at the University of New Mexico, was given the stapler question at an interview for a Microsoft internship position on April 18, 2003. His report: "I was being interviewed for a Software Design Engineer in Test summer internship position. The interviewer asked me to give 10–15 test cases. Many of the test cases I gave were related to quality, since I was interviewing for a position in quality control." He did not get an offer. These were some of his responses:

1. Does the stapler do what it is supposed to do? Staple pages . . . the simplest test case.

2. How many pages can it staple together?

3. Does it use the last staple pin properly or does it waste pins?

4. How good is the spring in the stapler—for example, does it rust?

5. Is the stapler light and easy to carry around?

6. Think like a devil—does it break if I throw it around?

7. Does it feature an easy-to-use staple-remover tool?

Extra credit for programmers: Here's a small, wicked program in pseudo-code that one candidate quickly whipped out in response to the challenge:

```
Function DoesStaplerWork()
    Interviewer.Hand.PlaceOnTable
    Interviewer.Hand.StapleToTable
    If Interviewer.Scream Then
        DoesStaplerWork = True
```

```
    ElseIf NOT Interviewer.Scream Then
        DoesStaplerWork = False
    End If
End Function
```

149 DESCRIBE BLUE TO ME

This puzzle is a favorite of Gerry Bollman, director of University Recruiting for Booz, Allen & Hamilton, in Cleveland.

Imagine I am blind. Describe blue to me.

Hint: There are four other senses besides vision.

If you have not considered this question before, now is the time to relax and think of a metaphor. Some candidates go into immediate panic mode and want to say something, anything, Bollman notes. "I like to see candidates who force themselves to be silent for a minute, take a step back, and think. For me, the ideal response has the candidate describe blue through analogies with the other four senses. For example, the candidate can describe blue in terms of taste or smell. The puzzle tests not only how creative people are, but how nonplussed they are about an unexpected challenge."

Here are two responses from candidates who have fielded this question. Each one attempts to answer the question using a metaphor or analogy.

Do you know George Gershwin's "Rhapsody in Blue"? You know the way you feel when you hear that first clarinet climbing the scale and then resolving into a pureness of tone that takes your breath away? That's blue.

Color is like the continuum between coolness and warmth. Every color reflects light differently. Light-colored clothing reflects more light than dark-colored clothing, so many people prefer to wear light-colored clothing in summer because it helps keep them cooler. Dark clothing tends to absorb more radiation and therefore heats up faster. Blue tends to operate as a dark color.

150 DESIGNING A HOUSE

Jabe Blumenthal, the original designer of Microsoft Excel, often asked this question of candidates. What can be simpler? But watch out! It's the simplest challenges that are the trickiest in which to shine because the risks of failing are so great.

Design a house.

According to Jabe Blumenthal, candidates would actually go up to the whiteboard and immediately draw a square. A square! "These were immediate No Hires," according to Blumenthal. "Not-so-smart candidates think that design is like painting: you get a blank slate, and you can do whatever you want. Blumenthal wanted candidates to demonstrate that they understood that design is a series of increasingly difficult trade-offs. The closer you are to the final design, the more difficult are the trade-offs."

The puzzle reminds me of an intelligence test educators used to give young children before they could read. The instruction was "draw a tree." If the child drew a tree that showed the tree's root structure (something important but hidden), the child was deemed more intelligent than one who started the tree at ground level.

"I will not hire someone who leaps into the design without asking more about who it's designed for," says Joel Spolsky, president of Fog Creek Software. In design questions, what are interviewers looking for? First, a sense of the candidate's curiosity. Great candidates will interrogate the interviewer for more information about the problem. Who is the house for? Is there a budget? Any special accessibility requirements? "Often I am so annoyed that I will give candidates a hard time by interrupting their analysis and saying, 'actually, you forgot to ask this, but this is a house for a family of 48-foot-tall blind giraffes,'" Spolsky says.

151 BILL GATES'S BATHROOM

There's an old saying that the customer is always right. That may be true, but the customer doesn't always know what he wants. That's why companies hire designers. Otherwise they could just ask the customers.

The main point of this very popular puzzle at Microsoft is to see if the candidate comes up with some bathroom features that Bill Gates wants but hasn't thought of on his own. That's why they are hiring you to design his bathroom. So start designing.

How would you design a bathroom for Bill Gates?

A good way to start is to sit down with the client (in this case Bill Gates) and listen to how he uses a bathroom. This conversation can get uncomfortable, but it's important not to gloss over the functionality of a bathroom. At the same time, the amenities, or "lifestyle factors," of a bathroom are just as important, especially to a client with an unlimited budget. In any event, you are supposed to start with such mundane matters as a budget and deadlines.

Then there would be a process of rapid iteration designing. You would show Gates your preliminary designs. He would comment and add some of his own ideas. The design would go through many cycles of revision. This is standard design process and should not be ignored.

You are also supposed to tilt toward a "smart" bathroom. Everyone knows that this particular client has a thing for adding computer intelligence to everything. So you might mention "smart" medicine cabinets that keep tabs on the expiration dates of prescription medicines and can order replacements for toothpaste and other items as inventory gets depleted. More elaborate designs suggest a toilet that analyzes samples to monitor the user's cholesterol and other health factors, generating reports and sending reports to the user's physician. Other designs feature IP-enabled toilet paper holders so the occupant is never inconvenienced by running out of toilet paper. By the way, even with all the talk of the "paperless" office, no one has yet proposed a paperless bathroom.

Microsoft interviewers have heard all of these gizmos (e.g., automatically flushing toilets), so if you want to get mileage out of this question, approach it the way the poet Emily Dickinson described telling a story: "tell the truth but tell it slant." Keep your design imagination grounded, but let it fly. Microsoft recruiters offer these three features as the types of responses that make them sit up and take notice:

- The kind of notepad that affixes to car windshields but designed for the bathroom. Better yet, make it a hands-free, voice-response notepad so the occupant can immediately preserve a precious idea by activating the device, perhaps with a code word, and then saying it aloud. The device automatically e-mails the message to the occupant's mailbox.

- A system to personalize the bathroom, depending on the occupant and his or her preferences. Akin to automobiles that "know" who opens the car door and automatically adjust seats, radio, and temperature controls, this system would adjust bathroom attributes such as ambient lighting, shower water temperature, toilet seat height, shampoo dispensers, etc., to the preferences of the occupant.

- A mirror that doesn't reverse left and right (see puzzle 14).

152 VENETIAN BLIND

This is another opportunity to display stupidity disguised as creative overdesign. Don't go there. You're not designing for a Las Vegas penthouse suite. Keep it simple.

Design a remote control for a venetian blind.

A good place to start is by stating the parameters of your design. Who is the intended audience? What is the budget? After that it is good to review the two controls needed to manually operate a venetian blind. One control raises and lowers the blind. The other control adjusts the angle of the slats to admit varying amounts of light. Assuming a motorized mechanism to open and close the blinds, a remote control with two dials will emulate manual operations. But perhaps a bit more intelligence in the remote control will be useful.

The intelligence can address two attributes of blinds. First, the blinds serve varying purposes depending on the time of the day, the day of the week, and the needs of the people in the room. People adjust blinds to meet changing conditions. In the morning the blinds are raised to admit sunlight. In the afternoon the blinds are adjusted against the strong sunlight. Then blinds are lowered at night for privacy. The remote control might include some simple controls to allow programming of the blinds to open at, say, 8 a.m., adjust for the afternoon sun at 3 p.m., and then lower for the evening at 7 p.m. This program might be synchronized with a photocell control so that on cloudy days, the blinds would admit more light than on sunny days. But in most parts of the United States, at least, the time of sunrise and sunset changes seasonally. A photocell can address some of these concerns. A more ambitious design solution is to have the venetian blind download seasonal times and perhaps even weather information, and then adjust itself accordingly.

Given that different people have different preferences for lighting conditions, the remote control might be designed to recall three or four preference settings. Akin to the car seat settings of many luxury cars—where with a push of a button, a car's seat assumes the preferred position for individual drivers—this design would facilitate individual venetian blind settings for individual residents.

FACTS YOU SHOULD KNOW

To succeed with brainteasers, candidates need to be armed with facts and know how to use them to advance to a logical solution. Even though it is a global economy, most brainteasers are still U.S.-based. Here are the essential facts every job candidate should know:

1. Population of the world   6.3 billion

2. Population of the United States   300 million

3. Number of adults in the United States   200 million

4. Number of households in the   125 million
   United States

5. State facts

Largest area	Alaska
Smallest area	Rhode Island
Most populated	California
Least populated	Wyoming
Southernmost state	Hawaii

6. Number of cars per household in the   2.5 cars
   United States

7. Minimum wage in the United $5.15 per hour
   States (basic)

8. Conversion factors

Inches	2.54 centimeters
Miles	5,280 feet
Miles	1.609 kilometers
Meters	3.281 feet
Pounds	0.453 kilogram
Gallons	3.785 liters
Cups	8 ounces, 48 teaspoons
9. Freezing point of water	0 degrees C; 32 degrees F
10. Boiling point of water	100 degrees C; 212 degrees F
11. Absolute zero	−273 degrees C; −459 degrees F

In addition, try to read the newspaper the day of your interview. Some interviewers weave facts from the day's news into the puzzles they administer.

20 THINK-ON-YOUR-FEET QUESTIONS

These challenging interview questions are not really brainteasers, but they often feel that way. Like many brainteasers, these questions don't have right or wrong answers. They all demand that you think outside the box and consider what information the interviewer is really looking for.

1. What was the last product or service you saw that took your breath away?

2. What's the most significant compliment anyone has ever paid you?

3. Is the customer always right?

4. How would you finish this sentence: Most people are basically . . . ?

5. Have you learned more from your mistakes or your successes?

6. What's the unwritten contract between you and the people that report to you?

7. Are you the type of person that likes to make lists or strike items off lists?

8. What would you do if your boss gave you a direct order to pursue a policy that you disagreed with?

9. The business world is full of euphemisms. What's your current favorite?

10. Should all business relationships have fixed terms—that is, expiration dates?

11. Is there anything positive to be said about conventional wisdom?

12. What's more important to you, truth or comfort?

13. When is it better to ask for forgiveness than to ask for permission?

14. Is honesty *always* the best policy?

15. You want to go swimming in a pool. The water is a little colder than comfortable. Are you the type of person who jumps in, or do you wade in?

16. On what occasions are you tempted to lie?

17. There are two candidates for one job. They have identical qualifications in every respect. How do you decide?

18. What do you want to hear first, the good news or the bad news?

19. If you could organize the world in one of three ways—no scarcity, no problems, or no rules—how would you do it?

20. Tell me about yourself in words of one syllable.

ADDITIONAL FERMI PROBLEMS

A Fermi problem, named for Italian-born physicist Enrico Fermi, is a problem in which realistic estimations and order-of-magnitude calculations are essential. If someone told a physicist she wouldn't study classical mechanics "for all the tea in China," the physicist might be tempted to calculate roughly how much tea there actually is in China. Solving Fermi problems is a great way to work on analytical skills and out-of-the-box thinking that lead to physical insight. The delight of a Fermi problem is to think about what assumptions we make, how to make them as realistic as possible, how to estimate well, and how to put all these in the service of a straightforward mathematical calculation to arrive at the answer.

1. How much tea is there in China?
2. How many jelly beans fill a one-liter jar?
3. What is the mass in kilograms of the student body in your school?
4. How many golf balls will fill a suitcase?
5. How many gallons of gasoline are used by cars each year in the United States?
6. Approximately what fraction of the area of the continental United States is covered by automobiles?
7. How many frames are in a Walt Disney animated movie such as *Tarzan*?
8. What is the mass of a fully loaded cement truck?

9. If you were to stack a pile of one dollar bills corresponding to the U.S. national debt, how high would it reach? How much would it weigh? What would be the pressure on the bottom dollar?

10. What is the length in miles of the U.S. interstate highway system?

11. How many molecules come off a car tire with each revolution?

12. How many gallons of water move down the Mississippi River in one day?

13. How many piano tuners would you expect to find in the local telephone directory?

14. If you could get a penny for each time someone said "Ouch!" in the United States, how long would it take you to become a billionaire?

15. If all the ball-bearings in all the fishing reels in the United States were dumped into a single grain elevator silo, how tall would the silo have to be?

16. Pick a nearby tree. Estimate the number of leaves on the tree.

17. The mass of how many Honda Civics is equal to the mass of the water in an Olympic-size swimming pool?

18. How many hairs are on your head?

19. What is the weight of solid garbage thrown away by American families every year?

20. If your life earnings are paid out to you at a certain rate per hour for every hour of your life, how much is your time worth?

21. How many hot dogs will be eaten at major league baseball games during a one-year season?

22. How many pizzas will be ordered in your state this year?

23. How many bowls of gumbo are eaten in Louisiana in one year?

24. Estimate the number of square inches of pizza consumed by all the students at the University of Maryland during one semester.

25. When it rains, water would accumulate on the roofs of flat-topped buildings if there were no drains. A heavy rain may deposit water to a depth of an inch or more. Given that water has a mass of about

one gram per cubic centimeter, estimate the total force that the roof of the physics lecture hall would have to support if we had an inch of rain and the roof drains were plugged.

26. Estimate the total amount of time 19-year-olds in the United States spent during this past semester studying for exams in college (not counting finals).

27. In the 1989 Loma Prieta earthquake in California, approximately 2 million books fell off the shelves at the Stanford University library. If you were the library administrator and wanted to hire enough part-time student labor to reorder the books on the shelves in two weeks, how many students would you have to hire? (You may assume that the books just fell off the shelves and got a bit mixed up, but books in different aisles did *not* get shuffled together.)

28. If the land area of the earth were divided up equally for each person on the planet, about how much would each person get?

29. How many notes are played on a given radio station in a given year?

30. How many pencils would it take to draw a straight line along the entire Prime Meridian of the earth?

31. If all the string were removed from all the tennis rackets in the United States and laid out end-to-end, how many round-trips from Detroit to Orlando could be made with the string?

32. How many drops of water are there in all the Great Lakes?

33. How far can a crow fly without stopping?

34. How tall is this building?

35. Estimate the number of cars and planes entering the state at any given time.

36. How much air (mass) is there in the room you are in?

37. How long does it take a lightbulb to turn off?

38. How much energy does it take to split a two-by-four?

39. How much milk is produced in the United States each year?

40. If you drop a pumpkin from the top of a 10-story building, what is the farthest a single pumpkin seed can land from the point of impact?

41. How many flat tires are there in the United States at any one time?

AN ESTIMATION OF THE TEA-IN-CHINA FERMI PROBLEM

Assumptions

- There are 2 billion people in China.
- Each person in China drinks, on average, 2 quarts of tea per day.
- It takes 1 ounce of tea leaves to brew 2 quarts of tea.
- There is a three-month supply of tea on hand in China at any given time.

Calculation

(2,000,000,000 people) (1 ounce tea/person/day) (90 days) = 180,000,000,000 ounces of tea = 11.25 billion pounds of tea

PUZZLES INAPPROPRIATE FOR JOB INTERVIEWS

Many types of brainteasers and puzzles simply do not belong in a job interview. For a variety of reasons, candidates will consider the following types of puzzles as either frivolous or, worse, a "gotcha" trap. In any case, they will alienate the candidate and bring disrepute on the organization. The difficulties with the following types of puzzles range from relying on a trick to being too frustrating, too culture-bound, too dependent on a particular language, or too time-consuming to solve. If you have experience—good or bad—with job interview puzzles in the following categories, please let me know at jkador@jkador.com.

LATERAL THINKING PUZZLES

Generally, these puzzles do not contain sufficient information for the solver to uncover the solution. These puzzles take the form of a seemingly strange or bizarre situation. The challenge is to interrogate the interviewer with questions that can be answered by one of only three possible answers—yes, no, or irrelevant. Good puzzles of this type call on an ability to challenge cultural assumptions and to reframe the situation in radical ways. When one line of inquiry reaches an end, then another approach is needed, often from a completely new direction. This is where the lateral thinking comes in.

While lateral thinking puzzles may give interviewers good information about how open-minded, flexible, and creative a candidate is, there is no avoiding the inherent "gotcha" factor of the exercise. But the major downside is that the lateral thinking puzzles are never quite solved; they are merely guessed at. That's not to say that lateral thinking puzzles are not satisfying. The so-called elevator puzzle is one of the best known and most celebrated of all lateral thinking puzzles. Although there are many possible solutions that fit the initial conditions, only the canonical answer is truly satisfying.

A man lives on the tenth floor of a building. Every day he takes the elevator to go down to the ground floor to go to work or to go shopping. When he returns, if he is alone in the elevator he takes the elevator to the seventh floor and walks up the stairs to reach his apartment on the tenth floor. When he is with someone, he rides all the way to ten. When it's raining outside, he also rides to ten, whether he is alone in the elevator or not. He hates climbing stairs, so why does he do it?

Solution: The man is of such small stature that he cannot reach the button for floor 10. When he is not alone, his elevator mate pushes 10 for him. When it's raining, the man has an umbrella he can use to extend his reach.

LOGIC PUZZLES

Strictly speaking, logic puzzles require the construction of a grid to organize the clues. The clues take forms such as "Mr. Green lives between the model train enthusiast and the grocer, two doors from the blue house." From an assortment of such clues one must deduce such things as the color and order of the houses on the street, the owners' names, their occupations, and their hobbies. The puzzler isolates the solution by logical elimination of the possibilities. While these types of puzzles can speak to a candidate's fact-gathering and organizing abilities, they are generally too rote and too time-consuming to be appropriate for job interviews.

LIAR–TRUTH TELLER PUZZLES

Generally liar–truth teller puzzles invoke two varieties of creatures, otherwise indistinguishable, except that one variety always tells the truth and the other variety always tells a lie. These puzzles generally set up a situation that requires the crafting of a carefully worded question that logically elicits the information desired to address the situation. These puzzles can be devilishly tricky, and success at solving them surely points to a highly verbal, logical intellect. On the other hand, having a conversation about such a puzzle can be very frustrating because of all the "if" statements required in its solution. For example:

> In front of you are two doors. One door leads to the executive interview room and the other to an exit. Next to each door are identical-looking consultants, one from our company and one representing our rival. The consultant from our firm always tells the truth. The consultant from the rival firm always lies. You can't tell which is which by looking. You are allowed to ask one consultant one question to find out which is the door to the executive interview room. What question do you ask?
>
> *Solution:* The key is to craft a question that gives you the information you want regardless of whether the consultant tells the truth or lies. Veteran puzzlers know that the way to do this is through the use of conditional statements creating double negatives. One strategy is to point at random to one door and ask, "If I asked you whether this is the way to the executive interview room, would you say it is?"

MATH PUZZLES

Math puzzles that require little more than computation or the ability to crunch numbers through a formula are simply not as interesting as brainteasers. Forget any puzzle that requires more than elementary arithmetic, geometry, or probability. *Unless you're interviewing for rocket scientists, calculus doesn't belong in a job interview.* Unless the job at hand requires specific mathematical skills, success at math proves little. If the job does require math, an aptitude test is a better way to go.

TRIAL-AND-ERROR PUZZLES

There are a variety of puzzles that are inventive and entertaining, but they require more or less brute force in their solution. Besides generally taking too much time to solve, such puzzles offer little in the way of discernment for either the interviewer or the interviewee. A classic example of such a problem is the following letter-substitution sum, said to be the entire contents of a postcard sent by a college student to his father. Each letter stands for a numeral. The goal is to determine what are the numbers of the sum (and the first task is to decide that it really is a sum):

	S	E	N	D
	M	O	R	E
M	O	N	E	Y

Solution: The monoalphabetic cipher has a unique solution. For those who want to figure this puzzle out with the help of an online puzzle worksheet, log onto Crack A Puzzle Online at www.geocities.com/Athens/Agora/2160/puzzle01.html. The site offers dozens of other such crypto-arithmetic puzzles. The unique solution for SEND + MORE = MONEY is 9567 + 1085 = 10,652.

TRICK QUESTIONS

"Gotcha" questions can be fun, but they are not appropriate for job interviews. Interviewers need to understand that the power balance in job interviews is unequal. Besides not yielding useful information, trick questions can make candidates feel even more powerless. Thankfully, most interviewers left questions like this behind in sixth grade where they belong: "A plane crashes on the border between the United States and Canada. Where are the survivors buried? *Answer:* Survivors are never buried." Trick questions can take on a veneer of respectability, but they are still trick questions:

> Five men dig five holes 5 feet deep in five hours. How long will it take one man to dig a half a hole?
> *Solution:* There is no such thing as half a hole.

SERIES PUZZLES

These kinds of puzzles take the form of a series of apparently random letters or numbers, and the challenge is to identify the next number or letter in the series. There is, of course, an underlying rule or logic determining the series. Some series puzzles can be fun and even illuminating. Success at these puzzles points to a facile mind that can detect patterns, a skill that is no doubt useful in business. But series puzzles often revolve around a single theme or "aha" insight. Either candidates get the series or they don't. Some may be culturally or geographically biased. Their biggest limitation as puzzles is that they don't offer much opportunity to have a conversation with the candidate. Here's an example:

What is the next letter in this series: O, T, T, F, F, ____?

Solution: S for "six." The series spells out numbers, one, two, three . . .

Here's an example of a geographically biased series puzzle:

What is the next number in the series 14, 23, 28, 33, 42, 51, ____?

Solution: 59 for 59th Street. The numbers represent the streets corresponding to the stops on New York City's Lexington Avenue subway line.

WORD PUZZLES

Word puzzles administered in English are too dependent on language and culture and would discriminate against those whose first language is not English. Here's an example of a word puzzle I would consider inappropriate for a job interview:

Can you name a word that uses the vowels A, E, I, O, U in order?

Solution: Facetious.

ADDITIONAL SOURCES AND LINKS

For convenience, readers may link to these resources from the author's Web site, www.jkador.com.

ACE THE INTERVIEW

A comprehensive resource for interview questions, including a good section of brainteasers and suggestions for handling them.

   http://www.acetheinterview.com/index.html

ACCENTURE

Accenture is a global management consulting, technology services, and outsourcing company, with approximately 86,000 people in 48 countries delivering a wide range of specialized capabilities and solutions to clients across all industries. The New York–based consulting firm offers help for success on the case interview by providing three sample cases (unfortunately without answers).

   http://careers3.accenture.com/Careers/US/CampusConnection/
   AdvancedDegree/TheCaseInterview/cc_ad_smba_cis_L02.htm

BAIN & COMPANY BUSINESS CASES

The international management company famously uses business cases in its rigorous selection process. Its career Web site states: "We value the case interview process as a means for us to get to know each other better. It is a chance for you to show us how you think through a real business problem, and for us to give you an example of the kinds of work we see every day. For this reason, our interviewers prepare their interviews based on real cases and tend not to rely on brainteasers or theoretical problems." The Web site includes two interactive case studies.

http://www.bain.com/bainweb/Join_Bain/case_interviews.asp

BOSTON CONSULTING GROUP BUSINESS CASES

This strategic managing consulting firm includes four comprehensive business cases on the career pages of its Web site. The cases are constantly updated, but they typically require candidates to analyze business situations in the manufacturing, medical, and retailing sectors. Check out the information under "What can you expect in a BCG interview?"

http://www.bcg.com/careers/interview_prep/practice_cases.jsp

BRAINBASHERS

BrainBashers is a seemingly bottomless well for puzzles, games, and optical illusions, all with solutions. It adds five new puzzles each week.

http://www.brainbashers.com/

BRAINTEASERS.COM

Extraordinary collection of brainteasers, mind-benders, riddles, puzzles, and trivia with many links to commercial sites.

http://www.brainteasers.com

BRAINTEASER PUZZLES BY QBRUTE

Difficult puzzles appropriate for only the toughest interviews.

http://www.angelfire.com/empire/qbrute/

BRAINGLE

With more than 6,000 brainteasers, riddles, logic problems, and mind puzzles submitted and ranked by users, Braingle has the deepest collection of items. Categorized puzzles include letter equations, math, riddles, probability, rebus, situation problems, and series.

http://www.braingle.com/index.php

BRAINVISTA

BrainVista is the most comprehensive collection of educational and recreational brainteasers, puzzles, and riddles for everyone, sorted by difficulty level and type. The questions and problems that are presented on the site require you to think in order to get the answer, and they are a good way to increase your creativity and mind power.

http://www.brainvista.com/bv/index.php

CAPITAL ONE BUSINESS CASES

The leading credit card issuer in the world has extensive information on its career pages, including interviewing advice and exploration of in-depth business cases.

http://www.capitalone.com

CAR TALK PUZZLER

Every week on the popular NPR radio show *Car Talk* hosts, Tom and Ray Magliozzi, also known as Click and Clack, present a logic puzzle. This feature has proved very popular with listeners. These "curious little conundrums" sometimes actually have to do with the inner workings of cars. Usually, however, they are variants of the puzzles in this book, but delivered in the brother's inimitable, conversational style. The site is very useful for insights on informal ways to present brainteasers. The site includes an archive with statements of puzzles and their solutions in both text and audio formats.

http://www.cartalk.com/content/puzzler/

ELUZIONS

A Web site with richly categorized puzzles, riddles, and games. Puzzle lovers will find almost every type of puzzle represented.

http://eluzions.com/Puzzles/

THE ENIGMATIC WORLD OF PHILIP CARTER

An author in West Yorkshire, England, Carter is the author of more than 100 books of puzzles and trivia for adults and children. His first book was *Take the IQ Challenge*. With Dutch author Marcel Feenstra and Australian author Christopher P. Harding, Carter produced *The Ultimate IQ Book*, which was followed by a sequel, *The Ultimate IQ Challenge*, in 1994.

http://www.knowl.demon.co.uk/

FERMI PROBLEMS

Hampton University lists hundreds of Fermi problems, puzzles for which realistic estimation and order-of-magnitude calculation skills are essential. Interviewers who want strikingly clever Fermi problems on which to base their puzzles will find what they need here.

http://www.jlab.org/~cecire/garden/fermiprob.html

FUNDRUM MY CONUNDRUM

A family collection of puzzles and riddles by Benjamin Kovler.

http://www.fundrummyconundrum.com/

HIRING TECHNICAL PEOPLE

Johanna Rothman's blog features very astute commentary about interviewing technical candidates. It also features a cautionary tale about the difficulties of using brainteasers and puzzles in job interviews.

http://www.jrothman.com/weblog/htpblogger.html

HITEQUEST HIGH-TECH INTERVIEW QUESTIONS

Geared to electronics and computer engineers, this collection includes technical and brainteaser questions and answers taken from real job interviews. Hitequest also has technical articles, job-searching tips, and engineering jokes.

http://www.hitequest.com/

HOW TO ACE THE BRAINTEASER JOB INTERVIEW

The author of this book posts new and updated puzzles and links to other puzzle sites and resources at his Web site.

www.jkador.com

HOW WOULD YOU MOVE MOUNT FUJI?

How Would You Move Mount Fuji? Microsoft's Cult of the Puzzle—How the World's Smartest Company Selects the Most Creative Thinkers by William Poundstone (Little, Brown and Company, 2003) is an extended discourse on the history and practice of technical hiring using puzzles and mental challenges. Poundstone explains that Microsoft was not the first company to ask such questions, but it certainly popularized the practice. This is a skeptical book. The author debunks the validity of intelligence tests and points out that Microsoft's interviews are a form of IQ test, even though Microsoft does not admit that publicly. He even challenges the notion that puzzle-based interviews are more objective than traditional interviews—more black or white, right or wrong—and therefore less subject to interpretation by the interviewers. The problem, he notes, is that interviewers' evaluation of answers can be extremely subjective.

In the chapter "How to Outsmart the Puzzle Interview," Poundstone provides useful tips for candidates who are confronted with such puzzle questions. The best candidates walk a fine line between the problem and process. Creative thinkers make many false starts and continually waver between unmanageable fantasies and systematic attack. Poundstone explains that you have to figure out when your fantasies have become too unmanageable: "To deal effectively with puzzles (and with the bigger problems for which they may be a model), you must operate on two or more levels simultaneously. One thread of consciousness tackles the problem while another, higher-level thread monitors the progress. You need to keep asking yourself, 'Is this approach working? How much time have I spent on this approach, and how likely is it to produce an answer soon? Is there something else I should be trying?'" For more go to http://techinterview.org/index.html. Also, see Ole Eichorn's review of the book at http://w-uh.com/articles/030524-moving_Mount_Fuji.html.

INDUCTIS BRAINTEASERS AND BUSINESS CASES

Based in New Providence, New Jersey, Inductis is a global management consulting firm with interests in New Dehli, India. Its career page includes an extraordinarily detailed and valuable Interview Prep Guide that offers in-depth analyses of both classic brainteasers and business cases. Brainteasers include fairly rigorous challenges in economics, probability, math, and engineering. Business cases include how many golf balls are made in the world, why there is no light beer sold in England, how many stories should a skyscraper have, and why high-price airlines survive.

http://www.inductis.com/careers.html

INSTITUTE FOR SECURITY AND OPEN METHODOLOGIES

Pete Herzog, managing director of the institute, created the scenario puzzles used in this book in Chapter 3, puzzles 36–41. For more information on the scenarios, contact Herzog at pete@isecom.org

http://www.isecom.org/

THE INTERVIEW BRAINTEASER AND ITS DISCONTENTS

Joe Mabel, director of development at Lux, is one of the most respected innovators in software development. Mabel has taught advanced classes in C++, multithreaded programming, and the use of consensus methods in a software development context.

As one who over a 20-year career has been on both sides of the interviewing table literally hundreds of times, Mabel is a vocal critic of using puzzles and brainteasers to select programmers. In a long essay called "The Interview Brainteaser and Its Discontents," Mabel argues that too much can go wrong with such puzzles. The article draws on actual interviews to demonstrate how badly these things often go. Mabel also includes advice for candidates on how to handle puzzles when they come up.

http://www.speakeasy.org/~jmabel/

LLOYD KING PUZZLES

A site maintained by the author of *Test Your Creative Thinking and Puzzles for the High IQ* (Kogan-Page, 2003). This book of 250 original lateral puzzles, including two creative thinking tests, aims to encourage readers to think creatively. The puzzles encourage unusual and unexpected associations, patterns, and connections.

http://www.ahapuzzles.com/

MCKINSEY & COMPANY CASE STUDY TIPS

The Boston-based consulting firm gives applicants a wealth of information about why it uses business case problems. It also offers suggestions and provides an online case study that applicants can take to get a feel for what they might get in a real interview.

http://www.mckinsey.com/careers/apply/interviewingtips/casestudy/

MICROSOFT CORPORATION

Ironically, Microsoft's career pages do not offer a wealth of information about its interviewing practices or how candidates should prepare.

http://www.microsoft.com/college/joinus/tips.asp

It does provide a few hints about résumés and interviewing at Microsoft here.

http://www.microsoft.com/careers/mslife/insidetrack/resume.aspx

MICROSOFT INTERVIEW QUESTIONS BY KIRAN

On his Web site, Kiran Kumar Bondalapati lists dozens of puzzles and brainteasers gleaned from hundreds of Microsoft interviews. Bondalapati, an expert in reconfigurable computing, no longer maintains this site and is cranky about visitors asking him for solutions. But the site includes many puzzles not in this book.

http://halcyon.usc.edu/ percent 7Ekiran/questions.html

MICROSOFT INTERVIEWS BY CHRIS SELLS

Over the years, Chris Sells has been collecting interview questions from Microsoft. "I guess I started this hobby with the intent of working there some day, although I still have never interviewed there myself," Sells says. "However, I thought I'd give all of those young Microserf wanna-bes a leg up and publish my collection so far. I've actually known people to study for weeks for a Microsoft interview. Instead, kids this age should be out having a life. If you're one of those—go outside! Catch some rays and chase that greenish monitor glow from your face!" The site includes reports from dozens of people who have completed Microsoft interviews (some successful, some not) and provides links to related sites.

http://www.sellsbrothers.com/

PROFESSOR TANGENT

This well-organized Web site includes logic puzzles, brainteasers, games, and humor.

http://www.professortangent.org/index.shtml

PROUDLY SERVING MY CORPORATE MASTERS

In *Proudly Serving My Corporate Masters: What I Learned from Ten Years as a Microsoft Programmer* (Writers Club Press, 2000), Adam Barr takes the covers off what it's like to be interviewed by, selected for, and successful at Microsoft. Forget what you have read elsewhere. In *Proudly Serving My Corporate Masters*, a 10-year veteran of the front lines of the software development wars gives firsthand information on how Microsoft works internally: how Microsoft recruits and interviews people and the relationships between programming teams and the rest of the company.

http://www.proudlyserving.com/

THE PUZZLING WORLD OF BARRY R. CLARKE

A well-done site with extensive links to brainteasers, puzzles, a forum, articles, and brain tests. Clarke offers a number of original brainteasers.

http://barryispuzzled.com/

REC.PUZZLES ARCHIVE

The rec.puzzles archive is a list of puzzles, categorized by subject area. Each puzzle includes a solution, compiled from various sources, which is supposed to be definitive. This is the index of the rec.puzzles archive edited for HTML. Solutions to many puzzles are available.

http://rec-puzzles.org/

TECHINTERVIEW

Michael Pryor, a programmer at Fog Creek Software, was inspired by William Poundstone's book to organize this site of puzzles for interviewers as much as candidates. Pryor writes: "This site is about challenging yourself to new puzzles and problems. Do not be afraid that if a question you use appears here then it won't be worth asking anymore. First, people who come to this site to read the problems are the *type* of people you want to hire. They are the people who get excited about solving problems, and actively search out new problems to ask themselves." Pryor posts links to solutions a month after the problem is posted.

http://techinterview.org/index.html

TECHNICAL QUESTIONS

A comprehensive list of links to brainteasers plus sorted programming questions to test expertise in C++, operating systems, and data structures.

http://www.ics.uci.edu/~bbhattac/interview/
Interview percent 20Questions.html

WILLIAM WU'S RIDDLES

A rich store of hard-core, tech-interview-style riddles, not Gaussian elimination logic puzzle fluff, accumulated and updated regularly by William Wu. Although Wu disdains offering solutions, a reader's forum discusses solutions to many of the problems.

http://www.ocf.berkeley.edu/~wwu/riddles/intro.shtml

LIST OF PROBLEMS

About the Author

John Kador is the author of eight books, including *201 Best Questions to Ask on Your Interview*, *50-High-Impact Speeches & Remarks: Proven Words You Can Adapt for Any Business Occasion*, and *Charles Schwab: How One Company Beat Wall Street and Reinvented the Brokerage Industry*. The author's Web site, www.jkador.com, features additional brainteasers and links.